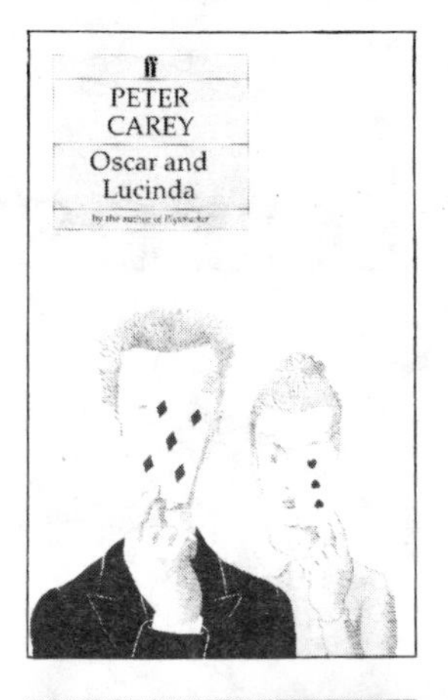

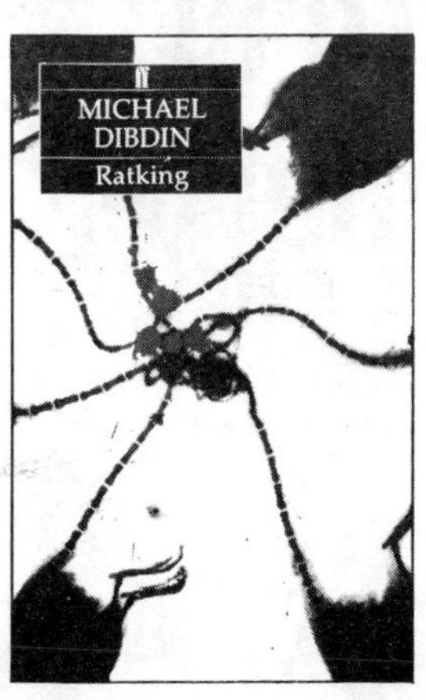

New Fiction from Faber

PETER CAREY
Oscar and Lucinda
£10.95

PAUL AUSTER
In the Country of Last Things
£9.95

MARIO VARGAS LLOSA
Who Killed Palomino Molero?
£9.95

ANDRÉ BRINK
States of Emergency
£9.95

MICHAEL DIBDIN
Ratking
£10.95

RODNEY HALL
Captivity Captive
£10.95

DESMOND HOGAN
Lebanon Lodge
£10.95

DAVID BROOKS
The Book of Sei
£9.95

UPAMANYU CHATTERJEE
English, August: An Indian Story
£11.95

MINETTE MARRIN
The Eye of the Beholder
£10.95

INSIDE INTELLIGENCE

24

Editorial and Subscription Correspondence: Granta, 44a Hobson Street, Cambridge CB1 1NL. Telephone: (0223) 315290.
All manuscripts are welcome but must be accompanied by a stamped, self-addressed envelope or they cannot be returned.

Subscriptions: £16.00 for four issues. Overseas add £4 postage.

Granta is photoset by Hobson Street Studio Ltd, Cambridge, and is printed by Hazell Watson and Viney Ltd, Aylesbury, Bucks.

Granta is published by Granta Publications Ltd and distributed by Penguin Books Ltd, Harmondsworth, Middlesex, England; Viking Penguin Inc., 40 West 23rd St, New York, New York, USA; Penguin Books Australia Ltd, Ringwood, Victoria, Australia; Penguin Books Canada Ltd, 2801 John Street, Markham, Ontario, Canada L3R 1B4; Penguin Books (NZ) Ltd, 182–90 Wairau Road, Auckland 10, New Zealand.

Granta 24, Summer 1988

ISBN 014-00-8605-6

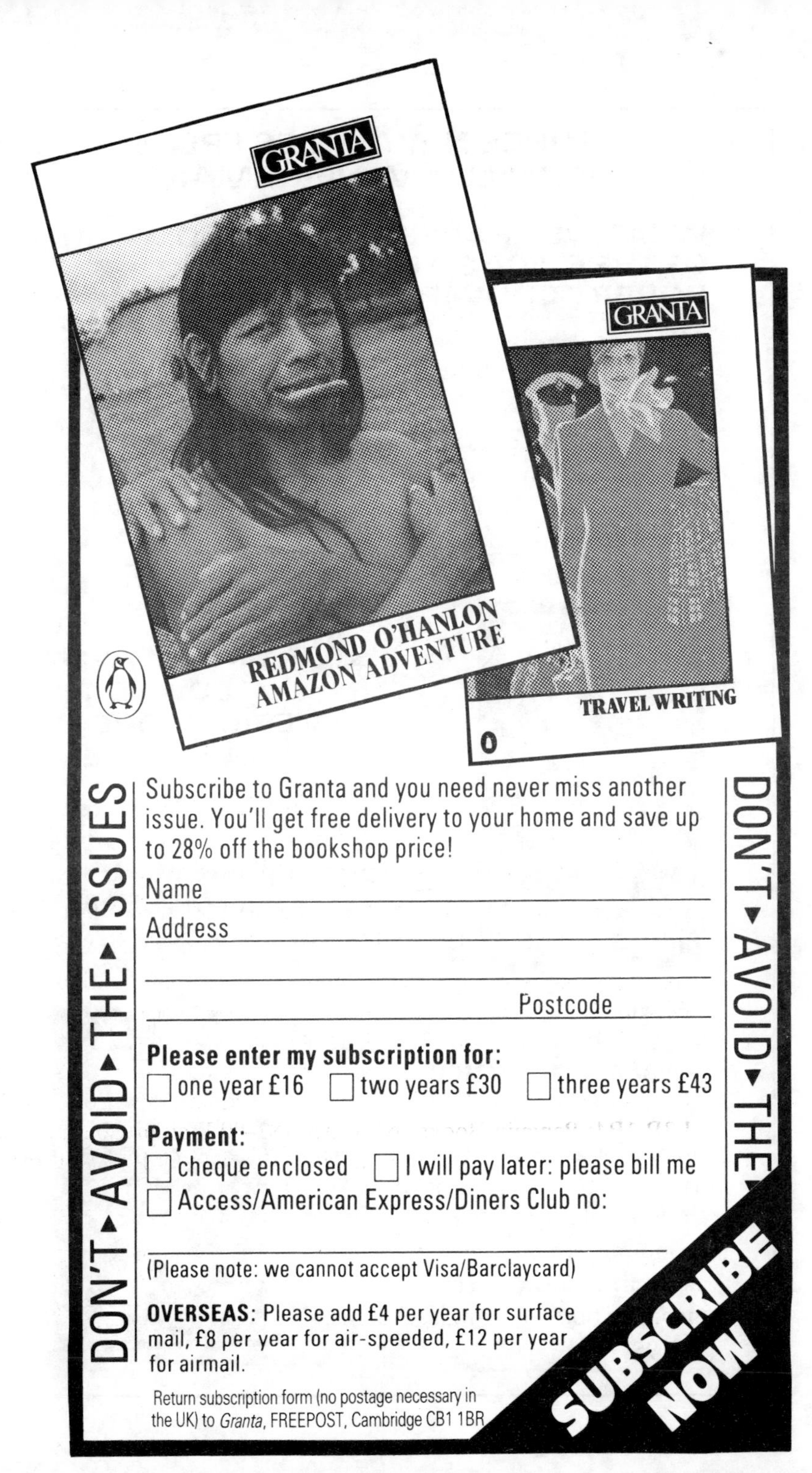
GRANTA
REDMOND O'HANLON
AMAZON ADVENTURE
GRANTA
TRAVEL WRITING
DON'T▸AVOID▸THE▸ISSUES
Subscribe to Granta and you need never miss another issue. You'll get free delivery to your home and save up to 28% off the bookshop price!
Name
Address
Postcode
Please enter my subscription for:
one year £16
two years £30
three years £43
Payment:
cheque enclosed
I will pay later: please bill me
Access/American Express/Diners Club no:
(Please note: we cannot accept Visa/Barclaycard)
OVERSEAS: Please add £4 per year for surface mail, £8 per year for air-speeded, £12 per year for airmail.
Return subscription form (no postage necessary in the UK) to Granta, FREEPOST, Cambridge CB1 1BR
DON'T▸AVOID▸THE▸
SUBSCRIBE NOW

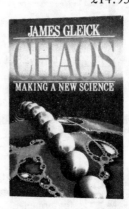

Contents

GRANTA

OBSERVATIONS

Photo: Hans and Judy Beste (Ardea)

The Albatross
Bruce Chatwin

For Bent Juel-Jensen

In *In Patagonia* I suggested that the albatross which hung from the neck of the Ancient Mariner was not the Great Wandering Albatross but a smaller black species: either the Sooty Albatross or the Black-browed. The Sooty is the likelier of the two. It is a streamlined bird that keeps to open sea. I think I saw one off the south-east coast of Tierra del Fuego. The Black-browed is everywhere, in the Magellan Straits and the Beagle Channel, and resembles a large Greater Black-backed Gull.

On the south side of the Beagle Channel is the Chilean island of Navarino, with its naval base at Puerto Williams. I hoped to walk around the coast and get a glimpse of Hermit Island, which is the breeding colony of the Black-browed Albatross. The wind and the rain drove me back.

East of the naval base there is a row of shacks in which live the last of the Fuegian Indians—the Indians Darwin mistook for the 'missing link'. He compared their language to the 'grunts of animals' being unaware that a young Fuegian spoke as many words as Shakespeare ever wrote.

Most of the Fuegians on Navarino are half-bloods. But I met Grandpa Felipe, who was said to be almost pure. He was a frail old man, mending his crab-gear. He had never been strong. He had watched his wife die. And all his children die.

'It was the epidemics,' he said—and whenever he said the word *epidemias*, it sounded as a mournful refrain.

A year and a half later, when *In Patagonia* was in press, I went to the island of Steep Holm in the Bristol Channel. My companion was a naturalist in his eighties. The purpose of our visit was to see in flower the peony that is supposed to have been brought here as a medicinal herb by monks from the Mediterranean.

I told my friend the story of how, in the nineteenth century, a Black-browed Albatross had followed a ship north of the Equator. Its direction-finding mechanisms had been thrown out of line. It had ended up on a rock in the Faroe Islands where it lived for thirty-odd years and was known as 'The King of the Gannets'. The Hon. Walter Rothschild made a pilgrimage to see it. Finally it was shot, stuffed and put in the Copenhagen Museum.

'But there's a new albatross,' the old man said. 'A female. She was on Bass Rock last year, and I think she's gone to Herma Ness.'

Herma Ness, at the tip of Unst in Shetland, is the ultimate headland of the British Isles.

From my flat in London, I called Bobby Tulloch, the Shetland ornithologist.

'Sure, she's on Herma Ness. She's made a nest among the gannets and she's sitting proud. Why don't you come and see her? You'll find her on the West Cliff. You can't miss her.'

I looked at my watch. It was nine o'clock. I had time to get to King's Cross Station before the night train left for Aberdeen. I put on my boots and packed a bag.

There was a hold-up on the tube. I almost missed the train. I ran down the platform at the last minute. The sleeping-car attendant was a craggy, white-haired Scot in a maroon uniform with gold braid. Beside him stood a small dark young man, waiting.

I was out of breath.

'Have you got a berth?' I asked.

'Aye,' said the sleeping-car attendant. 'If you don't mind sharing with that!'

He jerked his thumb at the little man.

'Of course not,' I said.

The man jumped into the upper bunk. I tried to talk. I tried English, French, Italian, Greek. Useless. I tried Spanish and it worked. I should have guessed. He was a South American Indian.

'Where are you from?' I asked.

'Chile.'

'I have been in Chile. Whereabouts?'

'Punta Arenas.'

Punta Arenas on the Magellan Straits is the southernmost city in the world.

'I was there,' I said.

'I come from Punta Arenas. But that is not my home. My home is Navarino Island.'

'You must know Grandpa Felipe.'

'*Es mi tío.*' He is my uncle.

Having exceptional powers of balance, the young man and his brother found work in Punta Arenas as refuellers of the light-buoys at the entrance to the Magellan Straits. In any sea they would jump onto the buoy and insert the fuel nozzle. After the fall of Allende, the brother got a job with an American oil company, using his talent on off-shore rigs. The company had sent him to the North Sea oil-field. He had asked for his brother to join him. They would each earn £600 a week.

I told him I was travelling north to see a bird that had flown from his country. The story mystified him.

Two days later I lay on the West Cliff off Herma Ness and watched the albatross through binoculars: a black exception in a snow-field of gannets. She sat, head high and tail high, on her nest of mud, on her clutch of infertile eggs.

ANTHONY CAVENDISH INSIDE INTELLIGENCE

Photo: Desmond O'Neill

Anthony Cavendish with Margaret Thatcher.

CENSORED

'Good heavens, old boy! It isn't the Russians we worry about; it's the British public we don't want to know about it.' Admiral Thomson, secretary of the D-notice committee, to Tom Driberg, MP, in 1956.

Last night, George Kennedy Young, a former deputy director of MI6, who wrote the foreword to 'Inside Intelligence', said: 'If Cavendish has broken the Official Secrets Act, then he should be prosecuted. But he hasn't, and the Government should not abuse injunctions in their attempts to censor information which is 30 years old.'

Sunday Times, 3 January 1988.

Photo: Dmitri Baltermants (Magnum)

2

I am perched atop a wooden cart loaded with hay, being pulled by a cow. The cow's name is Rosa, and every now and then she is struck on the side of the head by a peasant farmer. He is called Neeni, and we are on our way to his barn when we hear the other peasants shouting, *'Es git krig.'* 'It gives war.' And so it did. It was a Saturday, 2 September 1939.

We had lived in Switzerland since 1932, when my mother moved there following the death of my father. But with the prospect of war we returned to England, and my Swiss education was terminated. I remember the long train journey in April, 1940, regularly delayed by troop movements, and the crossing from Calais in which my mother and I crouched on the floor of our cabin in the dark, listening to the bombing.

Towards the end of the war, I volunteered for the Army. Having been educated in Switzerland, I was fluent in English, German, Swiss-German and French, and it was owing to my linguistic ability that I was sent to the School of Oriental and African Studies in London to learn Japanese. I was called away twice, early in 1945, to assist in interrogating captured Germans, and by VE day I had asked to be returned to my unit. I applied for a commission in the infantry for it was unheard of for someone under the age of twenty-five to be commissioned in the

Intelligence Corps. But during my training, I was summoned to the War Office for a further interview, and, as a result, it was decided that I should be commissioned as an intelligence officer. There was a six-week training course at the barracks in Aldershot, and then, after a short leave, I was posted to Cairo.

3

I arrived in Cairo in the summer of 1946 and was interviewed by an aged captain in Security Intelligence Middle East. I returned for a further interview, conducted, this time, by a young lieutenant-colonel who was to have a great influence on my life for the next thirty-five years. His name was Maurice Oldfield.

Security Intelligence Middle East, or SIME, was the regional office of MI5. I did not know that at the time, and Oldfield did not tell me. By the end of the interview, however, he did tell me that I would be working for him. I was being introduced to a different kind of army life. I was not to live in the military mess, but would share a flat, existing on the local economy. I was issued with the green security card. The card carried my photograph, and the text, in English and Arabic, advised that 'the bearer is engaged in security duties and is authorised to be *in any place at any time in any dress.*' It was signed on behalf of the commander-in-chief. It made me virtually a law unto myself; it was invaluable.

Oldfield's section was mainly devoted to Jewish terrorism and, in particular, overseeing the activities of the three illegal organizations in Palestine that were operating against the British: the Hagannah, the IZL and the Stern Gang. Within days of my arrival, early on the morning of 22 July, the IZL stole a number of vehicles, including a small truck loaded with milk churns, which they drove into the basement of the King David Hotel in Jerusalem, by way of the service entrance, unloading the milk churns and placing them directly under the offices of the High Commissioner's secretariat that, along with the military, operated from the hotel. The members of the IZL were dressed as Arabs and left on foot. The milk churns were packed with explosives that, just after midday, were detonated and all six floors of a corner of the King David Hotel collapsed. Ninety-one people were killed. The IZL claimed that it had telephoned warnings to newspapers and the police, but there was no evidence of any calls, although a newspaper office and telephonist in the Government secretariat had received calls after the explosion had taken place.

The atrocity of the King David Hotel stiffened the attitude of the military, which was, to a large extent, already pro-Arab and anti-Semitic. Lieutenant-General Evelyn Barker, the Army Commander, whose office was in the old city, published an order blaming the Jewish public for its passive support of the terrorists, adding that he wanted its members to be 'made aware of the contempt and loathing with which we regard them.' He ordered the cessation of social intercourse between the British soldiers and the Jews.

I flew up to Jerusalem in an RAF Dakota.

4

By 1947, it was clear that the Arabs would have to fight the Jews in Palestine. From the end of the war, arms had been stolen regularly from British military depots throughout the Middle East, but from 1947 the thefts increased. In 1947, the Arabs also began using German prisoners-of-war who were still held in Egypt: the Germans had experience with explosives; they knew military weaponry; and they were sympathetic to the Arab cause, if not actually anti-Semitic. The Arabs would organize the escape of the Germans from their prison camps and channel them along various underground routes to the Arab groups operating in Palestine. The stolen weapons, carried by camel across the desert, would end up in the Sinai, where the escaped prisoners-of-war would have been set up as instructors, training Arab units. It was clear to us that this underground network had to be infiltrated. And so, fluent in German, I agreed to be planted in a cell used for interrogating recaptured escaped prisoners to see if I could discover any leads which would enable us to close down the arms pipeline.

I was dressed for the part. I wore a blue denim shirt, shorts, a pair of wooden clogs and a home-made Afrika Korps peaked cap fashioned from the grey denim of the uniform. My cell mate,

Photo: Topham

Jerusalem's King David Hotel, seat of the British administration in Palestine, after it had been blown up by Jewish terrorists in 1946.

Willi Steinhauer, had twice escaped from his camp and had twice been recaptured.

For breakfast, we had bread with water, a thin stew for lunch and bread again in the evening. The cell was about ten feet wide and about ten feet high, and near the ceiling was the small gap to let in air. The prisoners were interrogated regularly, and after two weeks I had heard two useful pieces of information: the name of a café in Suez, the Kit-Kat, that was the start of an escape line to Arab Palestine, and the name of a prisoner at an RAF unit near Ismailia who was involved in the theft of military materials.

I passed on the information, and the next morning I was hauled roughly from my cell; soldiers shouted at me; I was kicked and told that, having discovered the crimes I committed during my last escape, they were taking me to court martial.

After a shower, a shave and a meal, I decided I would start with the escape line in Suez. The Kit-Kat was near the port, a low-life restaurant catering mainly to sailors. There were rooms upstairs, which prostitutes used by the half hour.

Some time later I arranged for the Suez military police to visit a number of restaurants in the area, showing a photograph of me in civilian clothes and asking the proprietors whether I had been seen and instructing them to inform the military police the moment I appeared. That evening I went to the Kit-Kat, and, in broken, guttural English, ordered a beer. A short while later the proprietor appeared. He was an Arab and asked me if I wanted another drink. He asked me where I came from.

I made to look a little awkward; I was half-German, I explained, and half-Swiss. I would be in Suez for a short while. I said nothing more.

The British military police, the proprietor said, were looking for someone who looked very much like me. He spoke quietly and wondered whether I would not prefer to go into his office. It would be embarrassing if the Military Police should return. We could have another drink.

I showed I was grateful but suspicious. All the same I joined him in his office, where he announced that he knew my identity: 'Paul Wagner, the escaped German prisoner-of-war.' He asked me about my military service, my age and details of the German Army. He wanted to help me, he said. I showed him a number of

Photo: Popperfoto

German prisoners-of-war.

battered back-dated letters addressed to me as Kaporal Paul Wagner. He said he would need two or three days to make the necessary arrangements; I also imagined that he would want to find out anything he could about me. I knew he'd come across the escape bulletin about me issued by the military police. Otherwise, there were no computers and little he could do.

For three days I waited. I stayed in a small room above the restaurant; the whores worked next door. A number of Arabs visited me. We talked about the German prisoners-of-war, about Palestine and about what would happen after the British left. The Arabs had been amassing arms since the end of the war, and even before that, during the war itself, but the weapons were often in bad condition—stored without proper care in wells and caves and wadis—and it was important that other German prisoners be contacted, especially those with access to arms—hand-grenades, ammunition and Sten guns. I was asked if I could help. There would be money and they would ensure I escaped.

I was given new clothes—a pimp's suit and a flashy tie—500 Egyptian pounds and a seaman's identity card showing that I was Norwegian. A meeting was arranged with one of the Arabs who had visited me, Mustapha, who lived ten kilometres to the south on the canal road.

I stopped at a small Arab tea bar sometimes frequented by Germans, and got into conversation with a couple of unshaven 804 drivers—the white-cabbed trucks of 804 Company were driven by Germans. The drivers saw through my Norwegian disguise and were keen to help a fellow German on the run. I met them three days in succession, on each occasion learning more about their duties, until finally one mentioned he frequently went to the RAF camp outside Ismailia.

There was good money, I told him, if arms could be stolen and smuggled out of the camp. The war had been over for two years; good money meant a way home. We agreed to meet a week later.

When we met, I was told that it would be possible to steal hand-grenades, detonators and also ammunition for .303 rifles. I asked how much and was told as much as a fifteen-hundredweight truck could carry.

I saw Mustapha later and we devised a plan: I would be given 1,000 pounds for the German drivers and 500 pounds for myself. On the following Wednesday, the truck would pull out from the RAF camp with the stolen goods and with only the driver aboard; he would then drive to a point four kilometres outside Ismailia, where I'd be waiting

Wednesday morning was hot and sticky, and the driver appeared at the time expected, his truck loaded with arms. I climbed in and instructed him to pick up an Arab boy who would be waiting one kilometre down the road: he would need a lift, having lost a shoe. We drove for another kilometre until we came across the young Arab boy. The boy told us to turn into a sand pit, just before Ismailia, where we transferred the arms to another truck. I handed over the money to the driver, and we went our separate ways.

I returned to town, to check with the Field Security Officer to see how the arrest had gone. But there had been no arrest: the shadowing of the German truck had failed and the Arabs had escaped with fifteen hundredweight of grenades and ammunition.

The arms were eventually located, but only after the boy had been spotted and dragged into a car and beaten and whipped with a rod across the soles of his feet until finally, amid his screams, he revealed that the arms were hidden in a dry well in a village outside Ismailia. All the Arabs involved in the arms pipeline were arrested. The boy was protected from recrimination, confined in the appalling conditions of an Egyptian prison.

That night I returned to the Kit-Kat. The proprietor left early in the evening—saying he would return immediately—and I had dinner. I feared that news of the Ismailia disaster would reach the café. I saw that I could end up another bloated corpse floating face down in the Canal.

I slept badly that night, waking early in a sweat. At about four in the morning, I crept down the stairs, pistol in hand, and left, suddenly believing that all was not well. I waited in the shadow of a shop doorway about fifty yards down the street and, as the sun began to rise, a large American car drew up outside the Kit-Kat and the café proprietor and two hefty men clambered out.

I was returned thereafter to my own identity. In that same month, however, I was travelling by Jeep with my driver up to Palestine from Kabrit in Egypt, and on our way there we were stopped by what we took to be British soldiers. But the four men who stopped us were terrorists, dressed in British khaki uniforms. They dragged us from the Jeep, which they then drove off the road into a wadi. I objected and was struck down by a blow to the face with a British rifle butt. It was fortunate that we were not wearing the badges of the Intelligence Corps, but those of the Royal Army Service Corps.

We were asked repeatedly where we were going, what unit we were from. They did not search our pockets and did not find my green card. They continued hitting us. We were both bleeding badly and were nearly unconscious. Then they stopped. And they fled.

The terrorists had spotted an armoured car on the road and wrongly identified it as an anti-terrorist patrol. We had come—the driver and I were to discover—very close to being kidnapped and executed.

There were three members of the IZL in prison, sentenced to hang by a British court, and, we later discovered, the IZL had made it clear that if the sentences were not commuted three British soldiers would be kidnapped and hanged in reprisal. On 12 July, two sergeants from the Intelligence Corps went for an evening drink in civilian clothes in Nathanya. They had with them a Jewish friend employed by the army. They were kidnapped by the IZL, and taken to a makeshift cell under the floor of a factory: there was a canvas bucket for a latrine and enough food and water for several days; there was an oxygen cylinder that they could breathe from.

On 29 July, the three IZL men were hanged. Within the next twenty-four hours the IZL took the two Englishmen—Sergeants Martin and Paice—out of their cell, tied their hands behind their backs with telegraph wire and then hanged them both. The bodies were taken to a eucalyptus grove and hung from two trees. A land-mine was buried directly under their bodies, which were found, still hanging, on the morning of 31 July; a party of troops were sent to collect the corpses: as the first sergeant cut the rope he jumped clear, the body fell on the mine and was blown into unrecognizable pieces. The explosion also brought down the tree on which the second body was hanging.

Anti-Semitic disorders broke out in England, and in Palestine some members of the police and army took the law into their own hands and beat or killed Jews. By the time control was reimposed, five Jews had been killed and many more injured.

I had been intended as the third victim—the IZL said they would hang three British soldiers, but only had two—and was saved by the timely arrival of the armoured car.

The killings increased, and it became clear that the problem was insoluble. At the end of 1947 Ernest Bevin's policy of non-participation was again approved, and it was decided that British rule would end in May 1948. From that time on the conflict was between the Arabs and the Jews, a conflict which continues to this day.

My time in the Middle East was ending. I had been there between July 1946 and July 1948, mainly in Egypt and Palestine; I had been involved in other activities, 'lent' out to other intelligence units: in one instance, interrogating illegal Jewish immigrants in Cyprus—it was suspected already that the Russians were infiltrating the refugees seeking to get to Palestine—and, in another instance, visiting Salonica in Northern Greece where communist deserters in the Greek Civil War were held.

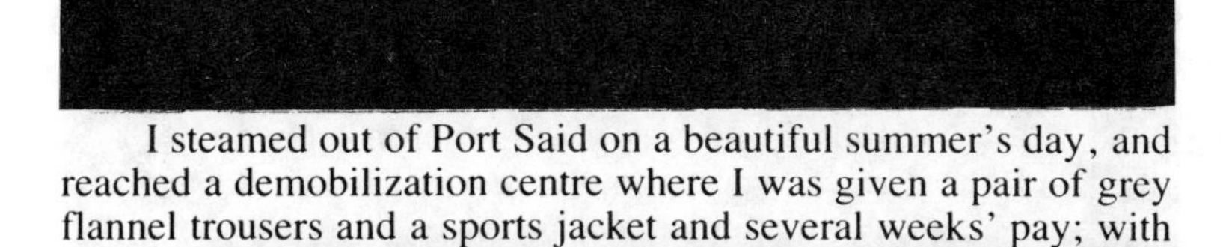

I steamed out of Port Said on a beautiful summer's day, and reached a demobilization centre where I was given a pair of grey flannel trousers and a sports jacket and several weeks' pay; with these,

5

Mr Alastair Cameron QC, for the Government, said he wanted to make it clear that material in the book ['Inside Intelligence'] was not a threat to national security as such, but it would be prejudicial to the interests of the Crown and therefore to national security in the broadest sense . . .

Lord Coulsfield, the judge, questioned Mr Cameron carefully about the information the court could be given on national security. Was he suggesting that publication be banned without giving any detailed reasons to the court?

'In an extreme case, yes,' Mr Cameron replied. He said the Crown would object very strongly to any examination of the blue-pencilled passages of the book to see whether they infringed national security. 'That's what worries me,' Lord Coulsfield said.

The Guardian, 17 February 1988.

6

[redacted], 3rd June, 1988
House of Commons,
London SW1

Dear [redacted],

I am aware of your comments in the media about the Peter Wright case and your general view about the obligations of officers in our Intelligence Services.

Rather than wait for you to make some further comment about me and my book, 'Inside Intelligence', I would like to set out certain facts for you.

I am not aware that you have served either in MI5 or MI6. What information you have, therefore, relating to the terms of service, methods of recruitment and the administration of the Security Service and the Secret Intelligence Service, is second-hand. That is to say, you have been told about them by parties representing them, or the Government which controls them.

I am sorry to say that the line the Government continues to use with regard to myself, is untrue.

The Attorney-General and the Treasury Solicitor have both been at pains to contend that officers who have served in either of the Intelligence Services, owe the Crown a life-long duty of confidentiality relating to their service.

Richard Norton-Taylor, writing in the *Guardian*, quotes George Kennedy Young, a former Vice-Chief of SIS, as saying that up until he left the Service in 1963, the term obligation of confidentiality was unknown. Norton-Taylor contacted a further four former SIS officers, who confirmed this to him. There is no question of the term having been in use, or the obligation having been a part of any understanding between the Service and its officers, when I left in 1953.

Photo: Popperfoto

Sir Stewart Menzies.

My book was not written to make money. As a former officer, loyalty must mean something to you. It does to me and I was not prepared to see my old boss, both in the Army and in SIS, smeared. I told SIS I was writing a book and I submitted it to them. They said nothing I had written could be published.

I published privately and subsequently in the Courts, two-thirds of the book was freed from the Injunction, including all of that part relating to my service in MI5.

The blue pencilling, to say the least, was arbitrary and in many cases, without logic.

Kim Philby's recent death reminds us that the paperwork and administration of the Intelligence Services, during and at the end of the War, was not efficient. It is clear now that Philby was never properly vetted. Similarly, other people who had been members of the Communist Party or practising homosexuals, were recruited into the Service without difficulty. There was certainly no agreement of employment and no undertaking was given, other than that required by the signing of the relevant portions of the Official Secrets Act.

The Attorney-General has stated more than once, that the Government in no way contends that I have breached the Official Secrets Act. That being so, and not having given any undertaking of confidentiality, it is clear that the Injunctions that have been taken out against newspapers to prevent them quoting anything I have said, are no more than a gagging procedure. The next step, as you know, is the Appeal to the House of Lords, which will be heard in the autumn.

Photo: BBC Hulton Picture Library

A Humber Super Snipe, an earlier version of which was used by British Intelligence in Germany.

Sir Dick White, when he took over as Chief of SIS, started to put his house in order, and officers who left the Service after his arrival, were required to sign a 'supplementary declaration', in which they undertook to do nothing which would be to the detriment of the Service, at the risk of losing their superannuation rights.

I have not made a penny out of the publication of 'Inside Intelligence'. Indeed, it has cost me approaching £5,000. Several thousand pounds, which newspapers were willing to pay me, I directed to the Century House Benevolent Fund. They have, however, rejected the money. I shall no doubt be able to find an ex-Services charity which is more sensibly run.

I hope you will find time to read this. You seem to be a regular commentator on intelligence matters, and I would like to know when I listen to you or read what you have said in future, that you knew the facts.

I am sending copies of this letter to [redacted] and [redacted], who are both interested in this saga.

Anthony Cavendish

Photo: Popperfoto

Photo: Popperfoto

7

CENSORED

A modified Type 43 *Schnellboot* of the kind used by British Intelligence.

The average depth of the Baltic Sea is fifty-four metres. It has no noticeable tide and deviations of eighty centimetres or more from the normal water level are very rare. In an average winter, between 100,000 and 200,000 square kilometres of the Baltic Sea are frozen.

Stills from the 1971 East German film *Rottenknechte* (*Band of Knaves*), which recreates the SIS-run operation to drop agents on the Latvian coast. Here, 'Cavendish' (right) briefs 'Klose', the German commander of the boat used to make the drops.

Radio Free Europe was founded in 1950, in Berlin, with an initial budget of ten million dollars. Among its sponsors are the American Sulphur Corporation; the Buffalo Rochester to Pittsburgh Railroad Company; Clark McAdams Clifford, director of the National Bank of Washington; C. Rodney, president of American Airlines; C.D. Jackson, publisher of *Time* and *Life*; Henry Ford II; General Motors; General Electric, Westinghouse; Chrysler and Esso. Its twenty-nine stations broadcast in sixteen different languages.

Since the British were attempting to contact these rebel groups, we had to take certain counter-measures. We decided to set up, in parallel to the real rebel groups, special units of our own agents who would pretend to be partisans. While these special units did not terrorize the local population, they still hid in the woods, and we supplied them with the necessary provisions, and finally succeeded in attracting the attention of the British secret service. An experienced intelligence officer, Albert Balodis, was in charge of these units, and he mixed with different partisan groups, and he met some of the British agents and eventually he was able to give them the impression that he was the leader of a huge underground organization.

And so the British landed their secret agents right into the midst of our special units, and we were able to keep all the British spies within our own net.

General Jan Janovich Vevers, former Latvian Minister of State Security.

British Intelligence Officer MacKibben: Mr Klose, are your men being well looked after?

Kapitän-Leutnant Hans Helmut Klose: No complaints, sir.

MacKibben: And what about yourself?

Klose: I'd rather be here than in a POW camp.

MacKibben: The modifications to your boat will be completed in about a week. I wonder whether you'd be interested in further co-operation with us?

Klose: Certainly, sir.

MacKibben: We need experts who are familiar with every nook and cranny of the Baltic coast.

Klose: What kind of duties should I expect?

MacKibben: We're setting up a Fishery Protection Service which will have certain special duties . . .

From *Rottenknechte* (*Band of Knaves*), East Germany, 1971.

Interviewer: Who was the commander of your boat?

Sigurd Kruminc: Hans Helmut Klose.

Interviewer: How do you know?

Kruminc: That's what he was called by 'John', the English secret service man.

Interviewer: What do you know about the boat?

Kruminc: It was an old Type 43 *Schnellboot*, but heavily modified. It was equipped with radar and weather-detecting equipment. The torpedo tubes had been converted to fuel tanks. The three diesel engines had been tuned to give 7,500 horsepower.

Interviewer: Mr Kruminc, what can you tell us about your route?

Kruminc: I took part in three landing missions. Each time we sailed along the Swedish coast, under Danish or Swedish flag, from Bornholm as far as Gotland. From there we headed due east towards the Latvian coast.

Interviewer: How did these landings take place?

Kruminc: Two oarsmen brought the two or three agents to shore in rubber boats. We were in radio contact with the speedboat. The radios and equipment were brought ashore first, then the oarsmen gave the agents the codes.

Kruminc was finally arrested after having been allowed to send 120 radio messages to HQ in England. He served fourteen years in prison—from *Band of Knaves.*

CENSORED

The money the spies brought with them was soon used up. Since they were going to starve, we set up an ambush on a tax inspector. The entire operation was carefully planned. I got out a large sum of money from our account and organized a wagon and horses. The roles of the tax inspector and his armed escort were played by two of our agents. The ambush was carried out by our unit in the presence of the British spies.

They had difficulty finding the money, and the armed escort had to point out that it was hidden in the sack of fodder at the bottom of the cart. We wanted to make it clear to the spies that ambushes of this kind were not without consequences. So we had one of our military units comb the woods 'in search' of the rebel group, and they had to leave their camp in a hurry. In their flight they left a good deal of their equipment behind, and all their food supplies. From then on they had to feed themselves on wild mushrooms and herbs.

German Welitschewski, State Security Officer, Riga.

Our social life was very gay in Berlin. I was delighted to discover that Claude Deshurst, of the magnificent Mercedes, whom I first met in Cairo was now in Berlin as a brigadier. He gave magnificent parties which, from time to time, got more than a little out of hand. Indeed Claude called me one morning to warn me that one of his guests, who had been dancing in Claude's fountain at a party, had had a photograph taken in a compromising position with a young German boy. Claude's friend—who was of use to us—was anxious that the photographs should be retrieved before they damaged his civilian career. A bit of quick action on the part of one of our agents soon brought the poor man relief and us a fair measure of gratitude.

In retrospect, there were a substantial number of homosexuals at work in intelligence in Germany. Even so, it came as a bit of a shock when two of my colleagues suddenly disappeared: one to prison and the other out of the Service for being caught *in flagrante* with young German boys. It was, in these cases, impossible to hush up the matter;

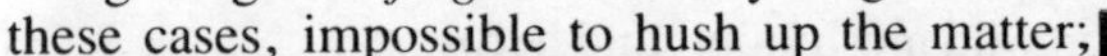

Photo: Popperfoto

US ARMY CHECKPOINT
YOU ARE
VOUS

8

Burgess packed up and left. We dined together on his last evening in a Chinese restaurant where each booth had 'personalised music' which helped to drown our voices. We went over the plan step by step. He was to meet a Soviet contact on arrival in London, and give him a full briefing. He was then to call on Maclean at his office armed with a sheet of paper giving the time and place of rendezvous which he would slip across the desk. He would then meet Maclean and put him fully in the picture. From then on, the matter was out of my hands. Burgess did not look too happy, and I must have had an inkling of what was on his mind. When I drove him to the station next morning, my last words, spoken only half-jocularly, were: 'Don't you go too' . . .

One morning, at a horribly early hour, Geoffrey Paterson called me by telephone. He explained that he had just received an enormously long Most Immediate telegram from London. It would take him all day to decypher without help, and he had just sent his secretary on a week's leave. Could he borrow mine? . . .

When I reached the Embassy, I went straight to Paterson's office. He looked grey. 'Kim,' he said in a half-whisper, 'the bird has flown.' I registered dawning horror (I hope). 'What bird? Not Maclean?' 'Yes,' he answered. 'But there's worse than that . . . *Guy Burgess* has gone with him.' At that, my consternation was no pretence.

Kim Philby in *My Silent War.*

Photo: Topham

East Berlin. A workman in Potsdamer Platz beats a Russian tank with a stick.

February 1945: First use of the term 'Iron Curtain'. Denouncing the Yalta Agreement, Josef Goebbels states that if the Soviet Union were to occupy eastern Europe then an 'Iron Curtain' would descend: 'Behind this curtain there would then begin a mass slaughter of peoples, probably with acclamation from the Jewish press in New York.'

August 1945: The United States drops atom bombs on Hiroshima and Nagasaki.

5 March 1946: Winston Churchill, as a private citizen, in Fulton, Missouri: 'Nobody knows what Soviet Russia and its communist international organization intend to do in the immediate future, or what are the limits, if any, to their expansive and proselytizing tendencies about the present position in Europe . . . From Stettin, in the Baltic, to Trieste, in the Adriatic, an Iron Curtain has descended across the Continent. Behind that line all the capitals of the ancient states of central and eastern Europe—Warsaw, Berlin, Prague, Vienna, Budapest, Belgrade, Bucharest and Sofia—all these famous cities, and the populations around them, lie in the Soviet sphere, and all are subject, in one form or another, not only to Soviet influence, but to a very high and increasing measure of control.'

12 March 1946: President Harry Truman announces the 'Truman Doctrine' to Congress: 'At the present moment in world history nearly every nation must choose between alternative ways of life. The choice is too often not a free one. One way of life is based upon the will of the majority . . . The second . . . is based

ANGLO-RUSSIAN
DEMARKATION LINE
АНГЛО-СОВЕТСКАЯ
ДЕМАРКАЦИОННАЯ
ЛИНИЯ
Englisch-russische

upon the will of a minority forcibly imposed upon the majority. It relies upon terror and oppression, a controlled press and radio, fixed elections and the suppression of personal freedoms. I believe that it must be the policy of the US to support free peoples who are resisting attempted subjection by armed minorities or by outside pressure. I believe that we must assist free peoples to work out their own destinies in their own way.'

July 1947: The National Security Act is passed, creating the Central Intelligence Agency.

19 December 1947: The National Security Council meets for the first time and adopts directive NSC 4/A, sanctioning covert action to defeat the Communist Party in forthcoming Italian elections.

25 February 1948: A Soviet backed *coup* installs a Communist government in Czechoslovakia.

18 June 1948: The National Security Council supersedes NSC 4/A with a new directive, NSC 10/2, authorizes the Office of Policy Co-ordination to run covert operations against the Soviet Union, 'including sabotage, anti-sabotage, demolition and evacuation measures, subversion against hostile states, including assistance to underground resistance groups, and support of indigenous anti-communist elements in threatened countries of the free world'—provided that, if such operations are 'uncovered, the US government can plausibly disclaim any responsibility.'

A two-seat version of the Russian MiG-15.

24 June 1948: The Soviet Union imposes a blockade on Berlin; the Berlin airlift begins.

14 April 1949: NATO is formed.

May 1949: The Berlin blockade is lifted.

Summer 1949: Kim Philby, top British intelligence officer and Soviet spy: 'I received a telegram from headquarters which . . . offered me the SIS representation in the United States, where I would be working with both the CIA and FBI . . . It took me all of half-an-hour to decide to accept the offer . . . I did not even think it worth waiting for confirmation from my Soviet colleagues.'

Albanian anti-communist émigrés land along the Albanian coast, dropped by parachute in an operation originating from the British base on Malta. Kim Philby: 'Shortly before my arrival in Washington the American and British Governments had sanctioned in principle a clandestine operation to detach an East European country from the Socialist *bloc.* The choice fell on Albania.' Some of the 'partisans' were given a show trial; most were shot.

SIS parachute Ukrainian 'freedom fighters' into the Soviet-held Carpathian mountains. They are caught and killed.

August 1949: The Soviet Union explodes an atom bomb.

January 1950: President Harry Truman orders the development of the H-bomb.

19 April 1950: The Soviet Union alleges that on 8 April a four-engined US bomber penetrated twenty-one kilometres of Soviet airspace south of Libava in Latvia and that it, after failing to comply with demands to land, was fired upon by a Soviet fighter. On 9 April American Air Force Headquarters in Wiesbaden, West Germany, announces that an unarmed US naval plane, with ten men on board, went missing after a routine flight from Wiesbaden to Copenhagen.

November 1952: The H-bomb is tested.

December 1952: After the CIA sends gold, weapons and radios to what it believes to be an anti-communist underground army, *Wilnosć i Niepodlenosć*, Polish radio broadcasts details of the operation, noting that WIN is controlled by Polish and Soviet intelligence.

5 March 1953: Stalin dies.

11 May 1953: Winston Churchill, again Prime Minister, proposes a summit to halt the decline in relations between the West and the USSR.

In order to resolve Anglo-American differences on the Ukrainian issue, CIA pressed for a full-scale conference with SIS, which was duly held in London in April 1951. Rather to my surprise, the British stood firm, and flatly refused to jettison the Ukrainan nationalist Stepan Bandera. The best that could be agreed, with unconcealed ill temper on the American side, was that the situation would be re-examined at the end of the 1951 parachute-dropping season, by which time, it was hoped, more facts would be available. Within a month, the British had dropped three six-man parties, the aircraft taking off from Cyprus. One party was dropped mid-way between Lwów and Tarnopol; another near the head-waters of the Prut, not far from Kolomyya; and a third just inside the borders of Poland, near the source of the San. In order to avoid the dangers of overlapping and duplication, the British and the Americans exchanged precise information about the timing and geographical co-ordinates of their operations. I do not know what happened to the parties concerned. But I can make an informed guess.

Kim Philby, SIS Liaison with CIA, 1949–51.

Photo: Topham

9

I was in the same position as I had been when I left the army. I needed a career and felt my best chance lay in journalism. I was helped in this by George Young, previously a journalist working for British United Press, but, even so, it was a full year before I was considered ready to go out on my own and was sent to Paris.

and I chose, for reasons now unclear to me, the Ambassadors of India, Poland and Yugoslavia as well as a number of others including the TASS correspondent, Ivan Saplin, whom I knew to be a KGB colonel.

The most charming man, however, was the Polish ambassador, Stanislaw Gajewski, and we used to meet for a drink about once a month. My friendship with him was to turn out to be enormously important, for that summer, the summer of 1956, marked the beginning of the unrest in the Soviet Bloc that culminated in the Hungarian Revolution. Rioting broke out in Poznań, and, while United Press had a stringer in Warsaw, it had no regular correspondent, nor did many others: the Polish authorities were refusing all press visas.

I visited Gajewski, therefore, who issued me with a visa immediately, without reference to Warsaw, and I left for Warsaw. Once there I succeeded in having an interview granted to me by the Prime Minister, Jozef Cyrankiewicz, which, with my being one of the few journalists from the West, was televised on Polish television and published the next day in the Party newspaper *Trybuna Luda*.

Many times during the next few months people would say of the rumblings in Eastern Europe that 'The Hungarians behaved like Poles, the Poles behaved like Czechs and the Czechs behaved like pigs.' The courageous Poles had shown their mettle at Poznań, but it was spontaneous and unprepared. But over the next ten weeks there were stirrings of unrest throughout the communist empire. I decided it was important to be in the East and so, with a permanent visa for Poland, I established myself as UP's Eastern European correspondent.

10

On 23 October 1956, a Tuesday, the lid blew off. But it was owing not to the Poles but to the Hungarians.

Basil Davidson of the *Daily Herald* had told me he was getting a lift to Budapest on a Polish Red Cross plane. On the evening of 27 October, I presented myself at Warsaw airport and told the duty officer that the Prime Minister's secretary had told me that a Red Cross plane was going to Budapest and that I should be on it. I urged him to phone the Prime Minister's residence for confirmation. The bluff worked and I found myself on a C-47 Dakota carrying 2,200 pounds of blood plasma that landed at five in the morning thirty-three miles south of the capital.

My first dispatch best describes what I saw.

> Soviet tanks and troops crunched out of this war-battered capital carrying their dead with them. They left a wrecked city, where the stench of death already rises from the smoking ruins to mingle with chill fog from the Danube river.
>
> I arrived here from Warsaw by plane, car and foot, walking the last five miles into the bleeding heart of this once beautiful city. As we approached the centre of Europe's worst upheaval since the last war I saw the full horror of devastation the revolution had brought.
>
> No sooner were we on the road north to Budapest than we ran into a massive southbound Soviet convoy headed by two armoured cars. Ten T-54 tanks, their red stars still visible through the grime of gunpowder, oil and blood, waddled behind, leaving Budapest.
>
> Then came numerous motorcycles and trucks.
>
> On the back of one tank lay the corpse of a Soviet soldier, his eyes staring vacantly back at the Hungarian capital. Other bodies were in the trucks. The Russian tank men, in their black crash helmets, looked tired and grim. They were retreating for the first time since they steam-rolled out of Mother Russia into Central Europe during World War Two.
>
> A Hungarian peasant spat on one tank as it passed

Budapest, 1956.

Photo: BBC Hulton Picture Library

127

him an arm's length away. The Russian crew did not notice. Hatred oozed from the Hungarians who silently lined the roadsides watching the Soviets evacuate Budapest. The Russians were nervous but alert. They manned their 100 millimetre tank cannon which were zeroed at the horizontal for firing straight ahead if necessary. And they held tightly to the handles of machine guns mounted in the tank cockpits and on truck tops.

I came across the first signs of fighting. Huge cannon holes punctured workers' houses. Windows were shattered. A strange music filled the air—the tinkling of broken glass being trodden on, driven on, swept aside. Telephone and high tension wires hung crazily and tangled like wet spaghetti as if a hurricane had passed through. We reached a railroad crossing. The crossing gates appeared ridiculous; they were so unnecessary. No trains would be running on that railroad for some time. Sleeping cars had been turned over as road-blocks. Their sides were stitched with machine-gun bullets, as if a giant sewing-machine had methodically worked them up and down, zigzagged and come back for a final floral touch.

We ran into convoys of Hungarian trucks pressed into duty as ambulances and flying Red Cross flags. The doctors looked like butchers, so blood-spattered were their once-white aprons. Trucks passed full of moaning wounded. Then a truck with a large sign proclaiming 'Dead Bodies'.

The stench was overpowering, and as we neared the city the acrid smell of cordite also assailed our nostrils.

We were now in the Budapest suburbs, and more and more Soviet troops and tanks could be counted hurrying the wrong way. I counted at least sixty Red Army tanks in one convoy. They looked like circus elephants lumbering one behind the other, twitching from side to side as their heavy steel trucks slipped on debris or an oil slick.

'Budapest City Limits', the sign said, and with it

came the distant chattering of machine guns. An impressive-looking Soviet tankman blocked the road and waved us into a detour. 'Mopping Up' operations were still going on. A tank gun coughed in the distance and a split second later came a muffled concussion that pressured the eardrums. The crack of rifles sounded from snipers who would prefer to die rather than give up.

The street now was so littered I had to abandon the car. I began walking through the suburbs into a city of death. There was Rakoczi Street, one of the main thoroughfares, leading down the bank of the gently flowing Danube. A Soviet tank was roaring down the street, and I jumped quickly into a doorway with visions of vile-tempered Russians who fired cannon at men, boys, women and children only a few blocks from here. It passed and the tingling in my stomach subsided. Hungarian women completely ignored the tank except for looks of such cold hatred that the emotion must have penetrated the steel side like X-rays. Trams, cars and battered trucks lay overturned in the streets as if by an irritable child who had scattered his toys with a blow of the hand.

Hungarian flags flew proudly from the vacant windows of shell-scarred houses. And all were minus the hated Communist Red Star which first appeared on the post-war Hungarian tricolour when the Soviets took over. The Red Star was scissored out, slashed out, burned out. Chalked signs were everywhere—'Russians go.' One brownish-reddish slogan on a wall appeared to have been written in blood. I passed a crowd happily hacking souvenir scraps from a giant bronze boot—part of the mammoth Josef Stalin monument toppled from its base last Tuesday night, cut with welders' torches and beaten to pieces—even to the walrus moustache.

A sort of cease-fire appeared to be in operation this morning, as Soviet troops slowly withdrew. Few here believe the 'Titoite' Government of Premier Imre Nagy, who was installed in the first dawn of the Revolution, can survive. Some solution will have to be worked out before the day is out, or the bloodletting will certainly begin again.

This proved to be the first communication out of Budapest for more than two days.

I teamed up with Basil Davidson, and we worked our way down Ferenc Street and into the Kilian Barracks. They were surrounded by tanks, and the air was filled with the sound of machine-guns and cannons and the dull, deadly thump of mortars. There was the whistle of small arms-fire and the roar of a Red Army self-propelled gun: its blast blew splinters of stone and grit into the doorway where we were standing.

A freedom fighter beside me insisted that the men inside the Kilian Barracks would never surrender. 'They will die there, or the Russians will go.' Those inside believed that the Russians would shoot them anyway if they came out; there was nothing to lose.

Basil and I returned to the car where we found a note pinned to the windshield: 'For the reporter of the United Press. We can give you this information: the members of the AVH [Secret Police] were all paid 10,000 florins [900 dollars] as well as their normal pay before the battles started. We found one of them and lynched him in the Ring Street and stuffed the money we found on him in his mouth.' The message was signed, 'From the two young architects you talked to at the graves of the fallen young in the Karolotzi garden.' In the Karolotzi Garden I had stopped at the graves of three fifteen-year-olds—two boys and a girl—shot dead by Russian troops.

Davidson and I later returned to the Kilian Barracks when there was a lull in the fighting. There we met the commander, Colonel Pal Maleter, already a legend of the revolution.

On Friday, 2 November, Davidson and I spent two hours in the parliament building with Deputy Premier Zoltan Tildy. We also met Anna Kethly, a right-wing social democrat imprisoned from 1950 to 1954, who was to become a minister in the new Hungarian government.

Tildy had received us wearing a well-pressed blue suit. Bodyguards with Thompson sub-machine guns stood watch by the doors. The Russians had withdrawn, and there were many who were starting to believe that the Hungarians might be able to

Cavendish with Pal Maleter, who became Hungarian Defence Minister after the 1956 uprising and was subsequently executed by the Soviets.

have their own way after all. But Zoltan Tildy and Anna Kethly both assured us that the Russians were lying: they were not pulling out. Although I had personally seen columns of Soviet tanks leaving Budapest, Tildy was sure that the withdrawal was merely window dressing.

'Several hundred tanks,' he said, had arrived from the Ukraine in the past forty-eight hours. And these were now 200 kilometres inside Hungary's frontier.

Radio Free Europe broadcasts continued to encourage the revolutionaries.

At four-thirty in the morning on Sunday, 4 November, I was wakened by a call from a Toronto Radio station wanting an eye-witness account of the situation in Budapest. Even as we spoke a terrific artillery barrage had started, and my room was lit by gunfire. I stared out of the window. An hour later, Soviet T-54 tanks began to pull up in the street outside the hotel.

The Red Army had returned, and Davidson and I retreated to the British legation to shelter there.

The Soviets had launched their attack at four-fifty that morning. A heavy Red Army battery perched on Gellert Hill, overlooking the city, blasted Hungarian rebel strong points. Tanks lumbered into the streets of the city, still only half-awake and unaware of the torture it still faced. Within an hour the Russians occupied all main centres and the bridges across the broad Danube.

A Soviet officer marched up to the main door of the Kilian Barracks and demanded entry. A rebel sentry opened the door and was shot dead on the spot. Red Army tanks then converged on the yellow stone building, already pock-marked from the earlier fighting. The tanks opened fire at point-blank range. Within an hour the barracks were blazing and more than 300 of the original 700 defenders were dead or dying.

The Russians destroyed a house to kill a single sniper. They pulverized the Korvin National Theatre. They fired at the historic Royal Palace, the Duna Hotel, and the Astoria Hotel. There was a clinic, directly in the line of fire, with 200 sick children inside. There were pleas from the doctors and nurses to spare the building. But the Red Army guns continued firing, right through

NX39

ADD SOVIETS, BUDAPEST XXX SIDE LIKE X-RAYS.

TROLLEY CARS, AUTOMOBILES AND BATTERED TRUCKS LAY OVERTURNED IN THE STREETS AS IF BY AN IRRITABLE CHILD WHO HAD SCATTERED HIS TOYS WITH A BLOW OF THE HAND.

HUNGARIAN FLAGS FLEW PROUDLY FROM THE VACANT WINDOWS OF SHELL-SCARRED HOUSES. AND ALL WERE MINUS THE HATED COMMUNIST RED STAR WHICH FIRST APPEARED ON THE POSTWAR HUNGARIAN TRICOLOR WHEN THE REDS TOOK OVER.

THE RED STAR WAS SCISSORED OUT, SLASHED OUT, BURNED OUT.

CHALKED SIGNS WERE EVERYWHERE--RUSSIANS GO HOME.

ONE BROWNISH-REDDISH SLOGAN ON A WALL APPEARED TO HAVE BEEN WRITTEN IN BLOOD.

I PASSED A CROWD HAPPILY HACKING SOUVENIR SCRAPS FROM A GIANT BRONZE BOOT---PART OF THE MAMMOTH JOSEF STALIN MONUMENT WHICH WAS TOPPLED FROM ITS BASE LAST TUESDAY NIGHT, CUT WITH WELDERS TORCHES AND BEATEN TO PIECES--EVEN TO THE WALRUS MOUSTACHE.

HZ715A

NX90

ADD SOVIETS BUDAPEST XXX WALRUS MOUSTACHE.

A CEASE FIRE APPEARED TO BE IN OPERATION THIS MORNING AS SOVIET TROOPS SLOWLY WITHDREW.

FEW HERE BELIEVE THE "TITOITE" GOVERNMENT OF PREMIER IMRE NAGY, WHO WAS INSTALLED IN THE FIRST DAWN OF THE REVOLUTION, CAN SURVIVE.

SOME SOLUTION WILL HAVE TO BE WORKED OUT BEFORE THE DAY IS OUT, OR THE BLOODLETTING WILL CERTAINLY BEGIN AGAIN.

HUNGARIANS WERE PITIFULLY FRIENDLY WITH THIS CORRESPONDENT. AS SOON AS ANYONE HEARD ENGLISH, A CROWD GATHERED.

MEN AND WOMEN SHOOK MY HAND AND POUNDED ME ON THE BACK.

"GOOD, GOOD," THEY SHOUTED.

I WALKED INTO AN ALREADY JAMMED HOTEL AND, WITH LITTLE HOPE OF SUCCESS, ASKED FOR A ROOM.

"IF YOU ARE WESTERN, WE'LL FIND YOU A ROOM EVEN IF WE ARE FULL," THE CLERK PROMISED.

I GOT A ROOM.

THE CURFEW IS STILL IN FORCE FROM 3 P.M. UNTIL 10 A.M. BUT PEOPLE LAST NIGHT DID NOT SEEM TO BE TAKING MUCH NOTICE OF IT.

REPORTS CIRCULATED HERE THAT REBELS IN THE WEST OF HUNGARY WERE MARCHING ON BUDAPEST. THE REPORTS COULD NOT BE CONFIRMED HERE.

BUT FROM THE GENERAL ATMOSPHERE IN THIS WRECKED CITY IT WAS APPARENT THAT THE REBELS WILL NOT GIVE IN UNTIL NAGY, TOO, IS OUSTED.

"WE HAVE COME THIS FAR," ONE HUNGARIAN SAID, "AND WE MIGHT AS WELL FINISH IT OFF."

THE PRICE WAS HIGH.

BLACK FLAGS OF MOURNING HUNG FROM MANY WINDOWS SIDE BY SIDE WITH THE RED-WHITE-GREEN HUNGARIAN FLAG.

PEOPLE ON THE STREETS, ON THE WHOLE, STILL APPEAR FAIRLY WELL DRESSED. THEY ARE NOT STARVING---YET.

BUT THE HORROR--AND TRIUMPH--OF THE PAST WEEK IS DEEP WITHIN THEIR EYES. THERE'S NO LANGUAGE BARRIER THERE--THE EYES SPEAK MOST ELOQUENTLY.

IT IS DOUBTFUL IF THE SOVIETS HAVE EVER CHURNED UP SUCH HATRED, ANYWHERE, ANYTIME.

FM1123A

U.P. UNITED PRESS ASSOCIATIONS · 220 EAST 42nd STREET, NEW YORK the clinic, as nurses and doctors sought to shield screaming children. In an hour the building was destroyed, piled deep with the bodies of children and staff. I will never know how many were killed, but it is certain that few escaped.

On Thursday morning, 8 November, I left Budapest by car to get the story of the battle to the West. I asked Basil Davidson and Ernest Leiser, an American CBS correspondent, to join me. We called at the Soviet Embassy to ask Ambassador Yuri Andropov to issue us with a safe-conduct pass and were told that a pass was unnecessary. As we left Budapest, heading north towards the Czech frontier, a Red Army sentry fired several rounds of machine-gun fire at us, but missed. We reached Leled, but, although we had valid Czech visas, the border guards refused to let us enter the country. We were accused of being counter-revolutionaries.

We spent the night with Hungarian railway workers in the village of Szob on the border—all pro-communists and all fiercely anti-Soviet. They made us welcome and shared their food with us. 'The West should have helped us more,' one of them told us. 'Radio Free Europe encouraged us, then the West let us down.' It was hard not to agree.

We left early next morning and took the ferry over the Danube at Esztergom. We drove on until we came to a road-block at Györ, where we were immediately arrested. The guards ordered us out of the car and everything was taken—papers, dispatches, cameras, and film. We were put under house arrest in a hotel and told that we would be held there until orders were received.

For two hours I was then interrogated by two KGB majors: What had I seen? Who did I talk to? Who sent me to Budapest? Why did I say I was only a journalist? The questioning was firm—sometimes hard—and repetitive, but I had the impression that the Russians themselves were not clear about what they expected from me.

On the third day, one of the KGB majors appeared and announced that we could go. We retrieved the car and our possessions and reached Vienna.

I left Hungary remembering the many instances of bravery I had witnessed. I saw how dedicated communists had come to see their belief in the Soviets violently destroyed: the ten days of ruthlessness and savagery that characterized the Red Army's response to a revolt within the Soviet system said more to the world about Soviet methods than any other event or any number of events had in the previous ten years. I took with me the memory of my meeting in the Soviet Embassy with Yuri Andropov on the day I left Budapest and his bland assurance for our safety. And I thought over and over again whether there was anything more I could have done and whether I had behaved in the right way when faced with danger.

Anthony Cavendish

Oldfield

I first met Maurice Oldfield in Cairo in the summer of 1946. He was a plump and owl-faced lieutenant-colonel with untidy hair and a rumpled khaki uniform. He wore spectacles and one sock dangerously lower than the other.

From then on Maurice and I were close friends. In fact, he was best man at the wedding to my French wife Odile. Maurice was brilliant at his job. He loved it and lived for it; Kim Philby referred to him as 'the formidable Maurice Oldfield'.

He had to wait until August 1973 to become head of MI6. He was an outstanding chief, and, when he retired, it would not be harsh or untrue to say he was like a fish out of water. He then accepted the job of security supremo for Northern Ireland and I was rarely to meet him without bodyguards in attendance. It was in the spring of 1980 that it became obvious to me that Maurice was deeply unhappy and seriously ill. My mother had died of cancer, and I thought I knew the signs.

On 12 June, it was announced that he had resigned his post for health reasons. The following day he begged me to come and see him. There were no lights on at all in the flat, and the sitting-room was thick with smoke. An ashtray was filled with the butts of the cheap cigarillos he smoked, and an almost-empty bottle of whisky was by his empty glass on a coffee table.

'Tony, I have been lying about my positive vetting,' he said. 'I have just resigned.'

I looked at him and saw an old and sick man, sick with sadness and with the cancer eating away inside him.

Photo: Topham

Maurice was concerned because he had failed to reveal various sexual adventures from his youth; the press smear campaign that followed alleged that Maurice was a compulsive homosexual. I knew for a fact that there were a large number of homosexuals in MI6. It is the sort of job which requires total dedication and makes heavy demands on a traditional family life.

Maurice was a modest and humble man, who came from a farming family in Derbyshire. He once told me sadly that it concerned him that the sort of woman he wanted to marry might find his family beneath her. He loved his family dearly. I do not know why Maurice never married. But I do know one thing for sure: he was not a homosexual.

Maurice Oldfield died on 11 March 1981.

Philby

It was in Beirut that I met Kim Philby ████. He frequented the bars at the Normandy Hotel and the St George's, and consumed large quantities of alcohol which seemed to have no effect on him. We invariably met for a pre-lunch drink, which, of course, always meant one thing: no lunch. A lunch-time drink with Kim Philby could last all afternoon.

Photo: BBC Hulton Picture Library

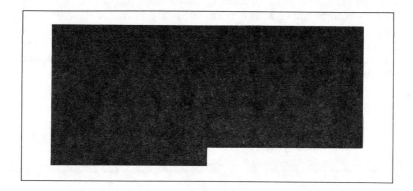

It is perhaps fitting to end this memoir with a story. In the bitter cold of the Russian winter, in a small village some hundreds of kilometres east of Moscow, during a howling gale and with darkness falling, a Russian peasant wanders home to his meagre village. Suddenly he stops as he sees a small bird on the ground, nearly dead from cold and privation. The peasant picks up the bird and warms it. The bird soon recovers and the peasant wonders what to do next. At that moment a herd of cattle come by and one of them drops a large dollop. Realizing that if he puts the bird in the steaming cow's dollop, the bird will stay warm until morning and then be able to fly away, he does this and then goes home. But a second peasant comes along after the first one has gone and hears the bird chirping happily to itself in the steaming mess. This peasant seizes the bird, breaks its neck and takes it home for supper.

This old intelligence story has three morals:

1. Do not believe that everybody who drops you in the shit is your enemy.
2. Do not believe that everybody who gets you out of the shit is your friend.
3. Whenever you are in the shit keep quiet about it.

Gilles Peress
Belfast

ERECTED
BY
JEAN STERRETT
IN LOVING MEMORY OF HER DEAR HUSBAND
WILLIAM JAMES DIED AUG 1957
ALSO HER DEAR MOTHER
MARGARET MATHEWS
DIED JULY 1957
BRANIFF

CARTLAN
IHS
DONNELLY
IN LOVING MEMORY OF MY DEAR HUSBAND
DANIEL
DIED 22ND NOVEMBER 1968
ALSO MY SISTERS
ALICE McCORMACK DIED 12TH MAY 1957
MAUREEN McCORMACK DIED 22ND AUGUST 1964
EILEEN DONNELLY DIED 25TH DECEMBER 1985
Pray for the soul of
JOSEPH CONNOLLY
DIED 11TH MARCH 1957
ALSO BRIGID CONNOLLY
DIED 29TH MAY 1968

WHITE

Philip Roth
His Roth

Nancy Crampton

One day in late October 1944, I was astonished to find my father, whose workday ordinarily began at seven and many nights didn't end until ten, sitting alone at the kitchen table in the middle of the afternoon. He was going into the hospital unexpectedly to have his appendix removed. Though he had already packed a bag to take with him, he had waited for my brother, Sandy, and me to get home from school to tell us not to be alarmed. 'Nothing to it,' he assured us, though we all knew that two of his brothers had died back in the 1920s from complications following difficult appendectomies. My mother, the president that year of our school's parent-teacher association, happened, quite unusually, to be away overnight in Atlantic City at a statewide PTA convention. My father had phoned her hotel, however, to tell her the news, and she had immediately begun preparations to return home. That would do it, I was sure: my mother's domestic ingenuity was on a par with Robinson Crusoe's, and as for nursing us all through our illnesses, we couldn't have received much better care from Florence Nightingale. As was usual in our household, everything was now under control.

By the time her train pulled into Newark that evening, the surgeon had opened him up, seen the mess, and despaired for my father's chances. At the age of forty-three, he was put on the critical list and given less than a fifty-fifty chance to survive.

Only the adults knew how bad things were. Sandy and I were allowed to go on believing that a father was indestructible—and ours turned out to be just that. Despite a raw emotional nature that makes him prey to intractable worry, his life has been distinguished by the power of resurgence. I've never intimately known anyone else—aside from my brother and me—to swing as swiftly through so wide a range of moods, anyone else to take things so hard, to be so openly racked by a serious setback, and yet, after the blow has reverberated down to the quick, to clamber back so aggressively, to recover lost ground and get going again.

He was saved by the new sulfa powder, developed during the early years of the war to treat battlefront wounds. Surviving was an awful ordeal none the less, his weakness from the near-fatal peritonitis exacerbated by a ten-day siege of hiccups during which he was unable to sleep or to keep down food. After he'd lost nearly thirty pounds, his shrunken face disclosed itself to us as a replica of my elderly grandmother's, the face of the mother whom he and all his brothers adored (towards the father—laconic, authoritarian, remote, an immigrant who'd trained in Galicia to be a rabbi but worked in America in a hat factory—their feelings were more confused). Bertha Zahnstecker Roth was a simple old-country woman, good-hearted, given to neither melancholy nor complaint, yet her everyday facial expression made it plain that she nursed no illusions about life's being easy. My father's resemblance to his mother would not appear so eerily again until he himself reached his eighties, and then only when he was in the grip of a struggle that stripped an otherwise physically youthful old man of his seeming impregnability, leaving him bewildered not so much because of the eye problem or the difficulty with his gait that had made serious inroads on his self-sufficiency but because he felt all at once abandoned by the masterful accomplice and overturner of obstacles, his determination.

When he was driven home from Newark's Beth Israel Hospital after six weeks in bed there, he barely had the strength, even with our assistance, to make it up the short back staircase to our second-storey apartment. It was December 1944 by then, a cold winter day, but through the windows the sunlight illuminated my parents' bedroom. Sandy and I came in to talk to him, both of us shy and grateful and, of course, stunned by how helpless he appeared seated weakly in a lone chair in the corner of the room. Seeing his sons together like that, my father could no longer control himself and began to sob. He was alive, the sun was shining, his wife was not widowed nor his boys fatherless—family life would now resume. It was not so complicated that an eleven-year-old couldn't understand his father's tears. I just didn't see, as he so clearly could, why or how it should have turned out differently.

I knew only two boys in our neighbourhood whose families were fatherless, and thought of them as no less blighted than the blind girl who attended our school for a while and had to be read to and shepherded everywhere. The fatherless boys seemed almost equally marked and set apart; in the aftermath of their fathers' deaths, they too struck me as scary and a little taboo. Though one was a model of obedience and the other a trouble-maker, everything either of them did or said seemed determined by his being a boy with a dead father and, however innocently I arrived at this notion, I was probably right.

I knew no child whose family was divided by divorce. Outside of the movie magazines and the tabloid headlines, it didn't exist, certainly not among Jews like us. Jews didn't get divorced—not because divorce was forbidden by Jewish law but because that was the way they were. If Jewish fathers didn't come home drunk and beat their wives—and in our neighbourhood, which was Jewry to me, I'd never heard of any who did—that too was because of the way they were. In our lore, the Jewish family was an inviolate haven against every form of menace, from personal isolation to gentile hostility. Regardless of internal friction and strife, it was assumed to be an indissoluble consolidation. *Hear, O Israel, the family is God, the family is One.*

Family indivisibility, the first commandment.

In the late 1940s, when my father's younger brother, Bernie, proclaimed his intention of divorcing the wife of nearly twenty years who was the mother of his two daughters, my mother and father were as stunned as if they'd heard that he'd killed somebody. Had Bernie committed murder and gone to jail for life, they would probably have rallied behind him despite the abominable, inexplicable deed. But when he made up his mind not merely to divorce but to do so to marry a younger woman, their support went instantly to the 'victims', the sister-in-law and the nieces. For his transgression, a breach of faith with his wife, his children, his entire clan—a dereliction of his duty as a Jew *and* as a Roth—Bernie encountered virtually universal condemnation.

That family rupture only began to mend when time revealed that no one had been destroyed by the divorce; in fact, anguished as they were by the break-up of their household, Bernie's ex-wife and his two girls were never remotely as indignant as the rest of the relatives. The healing owed a lot to Bernie himself, a more diplomatic man than most of his judges, but also to the fact that for my father the demands of family solidarity and the bond of family history exceeded even *his* admonishing instincts. It was to be another forty-odd years, however, before the two brothers threw their arms around each other and hungrily embraced in an unmistakable act of unqualified reconciliation. This occurred a few weeks before Bernie's death, in his late seventies, when his heart was failing rapidly and nobody, beginning with himself, expected him to last much longer.

I had driven my father over to see Bernie and his wife, Ruth, in their condominium in a retirement village in north-western Connecticut, twenty miles from my own home. It was Bernie's turn now to wear the little face of his unillusioned, stoical old mother; when he came to the door to let us in, there in his features was that stark resemblance that seemed to emerge in all the Roth brothers when they were up against it.

Ordinarily the two men would have met with a handshake, but when my father stepped into the hallway, so much was clear both about the time that was left to Bernie and about all those decades, seemingly stretching back to the beginning of time, during which they had been alive as their parents' offspring, that the handshake was swallowed up in a forceful hug that lasted minutes and left them in tears. They seemed to be saying goodbye to everyone already gone as well as to each other, the last two surviving children of the dour hat-blocker Sender and the imperturbable *balabusta* Bertha. Safely in his brother's arms, Bernie seemed also to be saying goodbye to himself. There was nothing to guard against or defend against or resent anymore, nothing even to remember. In these brothers, men so deeply swayed, despite their dissimilarity, by identical strains of family emotion, everything remembered had been distilled into pure, barely bearable feeling.

In the car afterwards my father said, 'We haven't held each other like that since we were small boys. My brother's dying, Philip. I used to push him around in his carriage. There were nine of us, with my mother and father. I'll be the last one left.'

While we drove back to my house (where he was staying in the upstairs back bedroom, a room in which he says he never fails to sleep like a baby) he recounted the struggles of each of his five brothers—with bankruptcies, illnesses, and in-laws, with marital dissension and bad loans, and with children, with their Gonerils, their Regans, and their Cordelias. He recalled for me the martyrdom of his only sister, what she and all the family had gone through when her husband the book-keeper who liked the horses had served a little time for embezzlement.

It wasn't exactly the first time I was hearing these stories.

Narrative is the form that his knowledge takes, and his repertoire has never been large: family, family, family, Newark, Newark, Newark, Jew, Jew, Jew. Somewhat like mine.

I naïvely believed as a child that I would always have a father present, and the truth seems to be that I always will. However awkward the union may sometimes have been, vulnerable to differences of opinion, to false expectations, to radically divergent experiences of America, strained by the colliding of two impatient, equally wilful temperaments and marred by masculine clumsiness, the link to him has been omnipresent. What's more, now, when he no longer commands my attention by his bulging biceps and his moral strictures, now, when he is no longer the biggest man I have to contend with—and when I am not all that far from being an old man myself—I am able to laugh at his jokes and hold his hand and concern myself with his well-being, I'm able to love him the way I wanted to when I was sixteen, seventeen, and eighteen but when, what with dealing with him and feeling at odds with him, it was simply an impossibility. *The* impossibility, for all that I always respected him for his particular burden and his struggle within a system that he didn't choose. The mythological role of a Jewish boy growing up in a family like mine—to become the hero one's father failed to be—I may even have achieved by now, but not at all in the way that was pre-ordained. After nearly forty years of living far from home, I'm equipped at last to be the most loving of sons—just, however, when he has another agenda. He is trying to die. He doesn't say that, nor, probably, does he think of it in those words, but that's his job now and, fight as he will to survive, he understands, as he always has, what the real work is.

Trying to die isn't like trying to commit suicide—it may actually be harder, because what you are trying to do is what you least want to have happen; you dread it but there it is and it must be done, and by no one but you. Twice in the last few years he has taken a shot at it, on two different occasions suddenly became so ill that I, who was then living abroad half the year, flew back to America to find him with barely enough strength to walk from the sofa to the TV set without clutching at every chair in between. And though each time the doctor, after a painstaking examination, was unable to find anything wrong with him, he none the less went to bed every night expecting not to awaken in the morning and, when he did awaken in the morning, he was fifteen minutes just getting himself into a sitting position on the edge of the bed and another hour shaving and dressing. Then, for God knows how long, he slouched unmoving over a bowl of cereal for which he had absolutely no appetite.

I was as certain as he was that this was it, yet neither time could he pull it off and, over a period of weeks, he recovered his strength and became himself again, loathing Reagan, defending Israel, phoning relatives, attending funerals, writing to newspapers, castigating William Buckley, watching MacNeil-Lehrer, exhorting his grown grandchildren, remembering in detail our own dead, and relentlessly, exactingly—and without having been asked—monitoring the caloric intake of the nice woman he lives with. It would seem that to prevail here, to try dying and to *do* it, he will have to work even harder than he did in the insurance business, where he achieved a remarkable success for a man with his social and educational handicaps. Of course, here too he'll eventually succeed—though clearly, despite his record of assiduous application to every job he has ever been assigned, things won't be easy. But then they never have been.

Needless to say, the link to my father was never so voluptuously tangible as the colossal bond to my mother's flesh, whose metamorphosed incarnation was a sleek black seal-skin coat into which I, the younger, the privileged, the pampered papoose, blissfully wormed myself whenever my father chauffeured us home to New Jersey on a winter Sunday from our semi-annual excursion to Radio City Music Hall and Manhattan's Chinatown: the unnameable animal-me bearing her dead father's name, the protoplasm-me, boy-baby, and body-burrower-in-training, joined by every nerve-ending to her smile and her seal-skin coat, while his resolute dutifulness, his relentless industriousness, his unreasoning obstinacy and harsh resentments, his illusions, his innocence, his allegiances, his fears were to constitute the original mould for the American, Jew, citizen, man, even for the writer, I would become. To be at all is to be her Philip, but in the embroilment with the buffeting world, my history still takes its spin from beginning as his Roth.

Tobias Wolff
Fortune

Our car boiled over again just after my mother and I crossed the Continental Divide. While we were waiting for it to cool we heard, from somewhere above us, the bawling of an air-horn. The sound got louder and then a big truck came around the corner and shot past us into the next curve, its trailer shimmying wildly. We stared after it. My mother said, 'Oh, Toby, he's lost his brakes.'

The sound of the horn grew distant, then faded in the wind that sighed in the trees all around us.

Quite a few people were standing along the cliff where the truck went over by the time we got there. It had smashed through the guard-rails and fallen through hundreds of feet of empty space to the river below, where it lay on its back among the boulders. It looked pitifully small. A stream of thick black smoke rose from the cab, feathering out in the wind. My mother asked whether anyone had gone to report the accident. Someone had. We stood with the others at the cliff's edge. Nobody spoke. My mother put her arm around my shoulder.

For the rest of the day she kept looking over at me, brushing back my hair and touching my cheek with the back of her hand. I saw that the time was right to make a play for souvenirs. I knew she had no money for them, and I had tried not to ask, but now that her guard was down I couldn't help myself. When we pulled out of Grand Junction I owned a beaded Indian belt, beaded moccasins, and a bronze horse with a removable, tooled-leather saddle.

It was 1955 and we were driving from Florida to Utah, to get away from a man my mother was afraid of and to get rich on uranium. We were going to change our luck.

We'd left Sarasota in the dead of summer, right after my tenth birthday, and headed west under low flickering skies that turned black and exploded and cleared just long enough to leave the air gauzy with steam. We drove through Georgia, Alabama, Tennessee, Kentucky, stopping to cool the engine in towns where people moved with arthritic slowness and spoke in thick, strangled tongues.

Every couple of hours the Nash Rambler boiled over. My mother kept digging into her little grub-stake but no mechanic could fix it. All we could do was wait for it to cool, then drive on until it boiled over again. (My mother came to hate this machine so much that when we reached Utah she gave it away to a woman she met in a cafeteria.) At night we slept in boggy rooms where headlight beams crawled up and down the walls and mosquitoes sang in our ears, incessant as the tires whining on the highway outside. But none of this bothered me. I was caught up in my mother's freedom, her delight in her freedom, her dream of transformation.

Everything was going to change when we got out west.

People in Utah were getting up poor in the morning and going to bed rich at night. You didn't need to be a mining engineer or a mineralogist. All you needed was a Geiger counter. We were on our way to the uranium fields, where my mother would get a job and keep her eyes open. Once she learned the ropes, she'd start prospecting for a claim of her own.

And when she found it she planned to do some serious compensating: for the years of hard work, first as a soda-jerk and then as a novice secretary, that had gotten her no farther than flat broke and sometimes not that far. For the break-up of our family five years ago. For the misery of her long affair with a violent man. She was going to make up for lost time, and I was going to help her.

We got to Utah the day after the truck went down. We were too late—months too late. Moab and the other mining towns had been overrun. All the motels were full. The locals had rented out their bedrooms and living-rooms and garages, and were now offering trailer-space in their front-yards for a hundred dollars a week, which was what my mother could make in a month if she had a job. But there were no jobs, and people were getting ornery. There'd been murders. Prostitutes walked the streets in broad daylight, drunk and bellicose. Geiger counters cost a fortune. Everyone told us to keep going.

My mother thought things over. Finally she bought a poor man's Geiger counter, a black light that was supposed to make uranium trace glow, and we started for Salt Lake City. My mother figured there must be ore somewhere around there. The fact that nobody else had found any meant we would have the place pretty much to ourselves. To tide us over she planned to take a job with the

Kennecott Mining Company, whose personnel officer had responded to a letter of inquiry she'd sent from Florida some time back. He had warned her against coming, said there was no work in Salt Lake and that his own company was about to go out on strike. But his letter was so friendly! My mother just knew she'd get a job out of him. It was as good as guaranteed.

So we drove on through the desert.

I didn't come to Utah to be the same boy I'd been before. I had my own dreams of transformation, western dreams, dreams of freedom and dominion and taciturn self-sufficiency. The first thing I wanted to do was change my name. A girl named Toby had joined my class before I left Florida, and this had caused both of us scalding humiliation.

I wanted to call myself Jack, after Jack London. I believed that having his name would charge me with some of the strength and competence inherent in my idea of him. The odds were good that I'd never have to share a class-room with a girl named Jack. And I liked the sound. Jack. Jack Wolff. My mother didn't like it at all, neither the idea of changing my name nor the name itself. I did not drop the subject. She finally agreed, but only on condition that I attend catechism classes. When I was ready to be received into the Church, she would allow me to take Jonathan as my baptismal name and shorten it to Jack. In the meantime I could introduce myself as Jack when I started school that fall.

My father got wind of this and called from Connecticut to demand that I stick to the name he had given me. It was, he said, an old family name. This turned out to be untrue. It just sounded like an old family name, as the furniture he bought at antique stores looked like old family furniture, and as the coat of arms he'd designed for himself looked like the shield of some fierce baron who'd spent his life wallowing in Saracen gore.

He was also unhappy about my becoming a Catholic. 'My family,' he told me, 'has always been Protestant. Episcopalian, actually.' Actually, his family had always been Jews, but I had to wait another ten years before learning this. In the extremity of his displeasure my father even put my older brother on the phone. I was surly, and Geoffrey didn't really care what I called myself, and there it ended.

My mother was pleased by my father's show of irritation and stuck up for me. A new name began to seem like a good idea to her. After all, he was in Connecticut and we were in Utah. Though my father was rolling in money at the time—he had married the millionairess he'd been living with before the divorce—he sent us nothing, not even the pittance the judge had prescribed for my support. We were barely making it, and making it in spite of him. My shedding the name he'd given me would put him in mind of that fact.

That fall I began catechism classes. Yellow leaves drifted past the windows as Sister James instructed us in the life of faith. She was a woman of passion. Her square jaw trembled when something moved her, and as she talked her eyes grew brilliant behind her winking rimless glasses. She could not sit still. Instead she paced between our desks, her habit rustling against us. She had no timidity or coyness. Even about sex she spoke graphically and with gusto. Sometimes she would forget where she was and start whistling.

Sister James did not like the idea of us running free after school. She feared we would spend our time with friends from the public schools we attended and possibly end up as Mormons. To account for our afternoons she had formed the Archery Club, the Painting Club and the Chess Club, and she demanded that each of us join one. They met twice a week. Attendance was compulsory. No one thought of disobeying her.

I belonged to the Archery Club. Girls were free to join but none did. On rainy days we practised in the church basement, on clear days outside. Sister James watched us when she could; at other times we were supervised by an older nun who was near-sighted and tried to control us by saying, 'Boys, boys . . .'

I was subject to fits of thinking myself unworthy, somehow deeply at fault. It didn't take much to bring this feeling to life, along with the certainty that everyone but my mother saw through me and did not like what they saw. I began to feel that Sister James knew all about me, and that a good part of her life was now given over to considering how bad I was. I became furtive around her. I began skipping archery and even some of my catechism classes. There was no immediate way for my mother to find out. We didn't have a telephone and she never went to church. She thought it was good for me but beside the point for herself, especially now that she was divorced and once again involved with Roy, the man she'd left Florida to get away from.

When I could, I ran around with boys from school. But they all came from Mormon families. When they weren't being catechized into their own faith, which was a lot of the time, their parents liked to have them close by. Most afternoons I wandered around in the trance that habitual solitude induces. I walked downtown and stared at merchandise. I imagined being adopted by different people I saw on the street. Sometimes, seeing a man in a suit come towards me from a distance that blurred his features, I would prepare myself to recognize my father and to be recognized by him. Then we would pass each other and a few minutes later I would pick someone else. I talked to anyone who would talk back. When the need came upon me, I knocked on the door of the nearest house and asked to use the bathroom. No one ever refused. I sat in other people's yards and played with their dogs. The dogs got to know me—by the end of the year they'd be waiting for me.

I also wrote long letters to my pen pal in Phoenix, Arizona. Her name was Alice. My class had been exchanging letters with her class since school began. We were supposed to write once a month but I wrote at least once a week, ten, twelve, fifteen pages at a time. I represented myself to her as the owner of a palomino horse named Smiley who shared my encounters with mountain lions, rattlesnakes and packs of coyotes on my father's ranch, the Lazy B. When I wasn't busy on the ranch, I raised German Shepherds and played for several athletic teams. Although Alice was a terse and irregular correspondent, I believed that she must be in awe of me and imagined someday presenting myself at her door to claim her adoration.

So I passed the hours after school. Sometimes, not very often, I felt lonely. Then I would go home to Roy.

Roy had tracked us down to Salt Lake a few weeks after we arrived. He took a room somewhere across town but spent most of his time in our apartment, making it clear that he would hold no grudges as long as my mother walked the line.

Roy didn't work. He had a small inheritance and supplemented that with disability checks from the Veterans Administration, which he claimed he would lose if he took a job. When he wasn't hunting or fishing or checking up on my mother, he sat at the kitchen table with a cigarette in his mouth and squinted at *The Shooter's Bible* through the smoke that veiled his face. He always seemed glad to see me. If I was lucky, he would put a couple of rifles in the car and we'd drive into the desert to shoot at cans and look for uranium. He'd caught the bug from my mother.

Roy rarely spoke on these trips. Every so often he would look at me and smile, then look away again. He seemed always deep in thought, staring at the road through mirrored sun-glasses, the wind ruffling the perfect waves of his hair. Roy was handsome in the conventional way that appeals to boys. He had a tattoo. He'd been to war and kept a kind of silence about it that was full of heroic implication. He was graceful in his movements. He could fix the Jeep if he had to, though he preferred to drive half-way across Utah to a mechanic he'd heard about from some loudmouth in a bar. He was an expert hunter who always got his buck. He taught both my mother and me to shoot, taught my mother so well that she became a better shot than he was—a real dead-eye.

My mother didn't tell me what went on between her and Roy, the threats and occasional brutality with which he held her in place. She was the same as ever with me, full of schemes and quick to laugh. Only now and then there came a night when she couldn't do anything but sit and cry, and then I comforted her, but I never knew her reasons. When these nights were over I put them from my mind. If there were other signs, I didn't see them. Roy's strangeness and the strangeness of our life with him had, over the years, become ordinary to me.

I thought Roy was what a man should be. My mother must have thought so too, once. I believed that I should like him, and pretended to myself that I did like him, even to the point of seeking out his company. He only turned on me once. I had discovered that my mother's cooking oil glowed like phosphorus under the black light, the way uranium was supposed to, and one day I splashed it all over some rocks we'd brought in. Roy got pretty worked up when he looked at them. I had to tell him why I was laughing so hard, and he didn't take it well. He gave me a hard, mean look. He stood there for a while, just holding me with this look, and finally he said, 'That's not funny,' and didn't speak to me again the rest of the night.

On our way back from the desert Roy would park near the insurance company where my mother, after learning that Kennecott really was out on strike, had found work as a secretary. Roy waited outside until she got off work. Then he followed her home, idling along the road, here and there pulling into a driveway to let her get ahead, then pulling out again to keep her in sight. If my mother had ever glanced behind her she would have spotted the Jeep immediately. But she didn't. She walked along in her crisp military stride, shoulders braced, head erect, and never looked back. Roy acted as though this were a game we were all playing. I knew it wasn't a game but I didn't know what it was, so I kept the promises he extracted from me to say nothing to her.

One afternoon near Christmas we missed her. She was not among the people who left when the building closed. Roy waited for a while, peering up at the darkened windows, watching the guard lock the doors. Then he panicked. He threw the Jeep into gear and sped around the block. He stopped in front of the building again. He turned off the engine and began whispering to himself. 'Yes,' he said, 'OK, OK,' and turned the engine back on. He drove around the block one more time and then tore down the neighboring streets, alternately slamming on the brakes and gunning the engine, his cheeks wet with tears, his lips moving like a supplicant's. This had all happened before, in Sarasota, and I knew better than to say anything. I just held on to the passenger grip and tried to look normal.

Finally he came to a stop. We sat there for a few minutes. When he seemed better, I asked if we could go home. Without looking at me, he nodded. He took a handkerchief from his shirt pocket, blew his nose, and put the handkerchief away.

My mother was cooking dinner and listening to carols when we came in. The windows were all steamed up. Roy watched me go over to the stove and lean against her. He kept looking at me until I looked at him. Then he winked. I knew he wanted me to wink back, and I also knew that it would somehow put me on his side if I did.

My mother hung one arm around my shoulders while she stirred the sauce. A glass of beer stood on the counter next to her.

'So how was archery?' she asked.

'OK,' I said. 'Fine.'

Roy said, 'We went out afterwards and shot a few bottles. Then we went tomcatting.'

'Tomcatting,' my mother repeated coldly. She hated the word.

Roy leaned against the refrigerator. 'Busy day?'

'Real busy. Hectic.'

'Not a minute to spare, huh?'

'They kept us hopping,' she said. She took a sip of beer and licked her lips.

'Must've been good to get out.'

'It was. Real good.'

'Terrific,' Roy said. 'Have a nice walk home?'

She nodded.

Roy smiled at me, and I gave in. I smiled back.

'I don't know who you think you're fooling,' Roy said to her. 'Even your own kid knows what you're up to.' He turned and walked back into the living-room. My mother closed her eyes, then opened them again and went on stirring.

It was one of those dinners where we didn't talk. Afterwards my mother got out her typewriter. She had lied about her typing speed in order to get work, and now her boss expected more from her than she could really do. That meant having to finish at night the reports she couldn't get through at the office. While she typed, Roy glowered at her over the rifles he was cleaning, and I wrote a letter to Alice. I put the letter in an envelope and gave it to my mother to mail. Then I went to bed.

Late that night I woke up and heard Roy's special nagging murmur, the different words blurring into one continuous sound through the wall that separated us. It seemed to go on and on. Then I heard my mother say, '*Shopping*! I was shopping! Can't I go shopping?' Roy resumed his murmur. I lay there, hugging the stuffed bear I was too old for and had promised to give up when I officially got my new name. Moonlight filled my room, an unheated addition at the rear of the apartment. On bright cold nights like this I could see the cloud of my breath and pretend that I was smoking, as I did now until I fell asleep again.

I was baptized during Easter along with several others from my catechism class. To prepare ourselves for communion we were supposed to make a confession, and Sister James appointed a time that week for each of us to come to the rectory and be escorted by her to the confessional. She would wait outside until we were finished and then guide us through our penance.

I thought about what to confess but I could not break my sense of being at fault down to its components. Trying to get a particular sin out of it was like fishing a swamp, where you feel the tug of something that at first seems promising and then resistant and finally hopeless as you realize that you've snagged the bottom, that you have the whole planet on the other end of your line. Nothing came to mind. I didn't see how I could go through with it, but in the end I hauled myself down to the church and kept my appointment. To have skipped it would have called attention to all my other absences and possibly provoked a visit from Sister James to my mother. I couldn't risk having the two of them compare notes.

Sister James met me as I was coming into the rectory. She asked if I was ready and I said I guessed so.

'It won't hurt,' she said. 'No more than a shot, anyway.'

We walked over to the church and down the side aisle to the confessional. Sister James opened the door for me. 'In you go,' she said. 'Make a good one now.'

I knelt with my face to the screen as we had been told to do and said, 'Bless me, Father, for I have sinned.'

I could hear someone breathing loudly on the other side. After a time he said, 'Well?'

I folded my hands together and closed my eyes and waited for something to present itself.

'You seem to be having some trouble.' His voice was deep and scratchy.

'Yes, sir.'

'Call me Father. I'm a priest, not a gentleman. Now then, you understand that whatever gets said in here stays in here.'

'Yes, Father.'

'I suppose you've thought a lot about this. Is that right?'

I said that I had.

'Well, you've just given yourself a case of nerves, that's all.

How about if we try again a little later. Shall we do that?'

'Yes, please, Father.'

'That's what we'll do, then. Just wait outside a second.'

I stood and left the confessional. Sister James came toward me from where she'd been standing against the wall. 'That wasn't so bad now, was it?' she asked.

'I'm supposed to wait,' I told her.

She looked at me. I could see she was curious, but she didn't ask any questions.

The priest came out soon after. He was old and very tall and walked with a limp. He stood close beside me and when I looked up at him I saw the white hair in his nostrils. He smelled strongly of tobacco. 'We had a little trouble getting started,' he said.

'Yes, Father?'

'He's just a bit nervous is all,' the priest said. 'Needs to relax. Nothing like a glass of milk for that.'

She nodded.

'Why don't we try again a little later? Say twenty minutes?'

'We'll be here, Father.'

Sister James and I went to the rectory kitchen. I sat at a steel cutting table while she poured me a glass of milk. 'You want some cookies?' she asked.

'That's all right, Sister.'

'Sure you do.' She put a package of Oreos on a plate and brought it to me. Then she sat down. With her arms crossed, hands hidden in her sleeves, she watched me eat and drink. Finally she said, 'What happened, then? Cat get your tongue?'

'Yes, Sister.'

'There's nothing to be afraid of.'

'I know.'

'Maybe you're just thinking of it wrong,' she said.

I stared at my hands on the table-top.

'I forgot to give you a napkin,' she said. 'Go on and lick them. Don't be shy.'

She waited until I looked up, and when I did I saw that she was younger than I'd thought her to be. Not that I'd given much thought to her age. Except for the really old nuns with canes or facial hair they all seemed outside of time, without past or future. But now, forced to look at Sister James across the narrow space of this gleaming table, I saw her differently. I saw an anxious woman of about my mother's age who wanted to help me without knowing what kind of help I needed. Her goodwill worked strongly on me. My eyes burned and my throat swelled up. I would have surrendered to her if only I'd known how.

'It probably isn't as bad as you think it is,' Sister James said. 'Whatever it is, someday you'll look back and you'll see that it was natural. But you've got to bring it to the light. Keeping it in the dark is what makes it feel so bad.' She added, 'I'm not asking you to tell me, understand. That's not my place. I'm just saying that we all go through these things.'

Sister James leaned forward over the table. 'When I was your age,' she said, 'maybe even a little older, I used to go through my father's wallet while he was taking his bath at night. I didn't take bills, just pennies and nickels, maybe a dime. Nothing he'd miss. My father would have given me the money if I'd asked for it. But I preferred to steal it. Stealing from him made me feel awful, but I did it all the same.'

She looked down at the table-top. 'I was a backbiter, too. Whenever I was with one friend I would say terrible things about my other friends, and then turn around and do the same thing to the one I had just been with. I knew what I was doing, too. I hated myself for it, I really did, but that didn't stop me. I used to wish that my mother and my brothers would die in a car crash so I could grow up with just my father and have everyone feel sorry for me.'

Sister James shook her head. 'I had all these bad thoughts I didn't want to let go of. Know what I mean?'

I nodded, and presented her with an expression that was meant to register dawning comprehension.

'Good!' she said. She slapped her palms down on the table. 'Ready to try again?'

I said that I was.

Sister James led me back to the confessional. I knelt and began again: 'Bless me, Father, for—'

'All right,' he said. 'We've been here before. Just talk plain.'

'Yes, Father.'

Again I closed my eyes over my folded hands.

'Come come,' he said, with a certain sharpness.

'Yes, Father.' I bent close to the screen and whispered, 'Father, I steal.'

He was silent for a moment. Then he said, 'What do you steal?'

'I steal money, Father. From my mother's purse when she's in the shower.'

'How long have you been doing this?'

I didn't answer.

'Well?' he said. 'A week? A year? Two years?'

I chose the one in the middle. 'A year.'

'A year,' he repeated. 'That won't do. You have to stop. Do you intend to stop?'

'Yes, Father.'

'Honestly, now.'

'Honestly, Father.'

'All right. Good. What else?'

'I'm a backbiter,' I whispered.

'A backbiter?'

'I say things about my friends when they're not around.'

'That won't do either,' he said.

'No, Father.'

'That certainly won't do. Your friends will desert you if you persist in this and let me tell you, a life without friends is no life at all.'

'Yes, Father.'

'Do you sincerely intend to stop?'

'Yes, Father.'

'Good. Be sure that you do. I tell you this in all seriousness. Anything else?'

'I have bad thoughts, Father.'

'Yes. Well,' he said, 'why don't we save those for next time? You have enough to work on.'

The priest gave me my penance and absolved me. As I left the confessional I heard his own door open and close. Sister James came forward to meet me again, and we waited together as the priest made his way to where we stood. Breathing hoarsely, he steadied himself against a pillar. He laid his other hand on my shoulder. 'That was fine,' he said. 'Just fine.' He gave my shoulder a squeeze. 'You have a fine boy here, Sister James.'

She smiled at me. 'So I do, Father. So I do.'

Just after Easter Roy gave me the Winchester .22 rifle I'd learned to shoot with. It was a light, pump-action, beautifully balanced piece with a walnut stock black from all its oilings. Roy had carried it when he was a boy, and it was still as good as new. Better than new. The action was silky from long use, and the wood of a quality no longer to be found.

The gift did not come as a surprise. Roy was stingy, and slow to take a hint, but I'd put him under siege. I had my heart set on that rifle. A weapon was the first condition of self-sufficiency, and of being a real westerner, and of all acceptable employment—trapping, riding herd, soldiering, law-enforcement and outlawry. I needed that rifle, for itself and for the way it completed me when I held it.

My mother said I couldn't have it. Absolutely not. Roy took the rifle back but promised me he'd bring her around. He could not imagine anyone refusing him anything and treated the refusals he did encounter as perverse and insincere. Normally mute, he became at these times a relentless whiner. He would follow my mother from room to room, emitting one ceaseless note of complaint that was pitched perfectly to jelly her nerves and bring her to a state where she would agree to anything to make it stop.

After a few days of this my mother caved in. She said I could have the rifle if, and only if, I promised never to take it out or even touch it except when she and Roy were with me. OK, I said. Sure. Naturally. But even then she wasn't satisfied. She plain didn't like the fact of me owning a rifle. Roy said he had owned several rifles by the time he was my age, but this did not reassure her. She didn't think I could be trusted with it. Roy said now was the time to find out.

For a week or so I kept my promises. But now that the weather had turned warm Roy was usually off somewhere, and eventually, in the dead hours after school when I found myself alone in the apartment, I decided that there couldn't be any harm in taking the rifle out to clean it. Only to clean it, nothing more. I was sure it would be enough just to break it down, oil it, rub linseed into the stock, polish the octagonal barrel and then hold it up to the light to confirm the perfection of the bore. But it wasn't enough. From cleaning the rifle I went to marching around the apartment with it, and then to striking brave poses in front of the mirror. Roy had saved one of his army uniforms and I sometimes dressed up in this, together with martial-looking articles of hunting gear: fur trooper's hat, camouflage coat, boots that reached nearly to my knees.

The camouflage coat made me feel like a sniper, and before long I began to act like one. I set up a nest on the couch by the front window. I drew the shades to darken the apartment, and took up my position. Nudging the shade aside with the rifle barrel, I followed people in my sights as they walked or drove along the street. At first I made shooting sounds: kyoo! kyoo! Then I started cocking the hammer and letting it snap down.

Roy stored his ammunition in a metal box he kept hidden in the closet. I knew exactly where to find it, along with every other hidden thing in the apartment. There was a layer of loose .22 rounds on the bottom of the box under shells of bigger caliber, dropped there by the handful the way men drop pennies on their dressers at night. I took some and put them in a hiding place of my own. With these I started loading up the rifle. Hammer cocked, a round in the chamber, finger resting lightly on the trigger, I drew a bead on whoever walked by—women pushing strollers, children, garbage collectors laughing and calling to one another, anyone—and as they passed under my window I sometimes had to bite my lip to keep from laughing in the ecstasy of my power over them, and at their absurd and innocent belief that they were safe.

But over time the innocence I laughed at began to irritate me. It was a peculiar kind of irritation. I saw it years later in men I served with, and felt it myself, when unarmed Vietnamese civilians talked back to us while we were herding them around. Power can be enjoyed only when it is recognized and feared. Fearlessness in those without power is maddening to those who have it.

One afternoon I pulled the trigger. I had been aiming at two old people, a man and a woman, who walked so slowly that by the time they turned the corner at the bottom of the hill my little store of self-control was exhausted. I had to shoot. I looked up and down the street. It was empty. Nothing moved but a pair of squirrels chasing each other back and forth on the telephone wires. I followed one in my sights. Finally it stopped for a moment and I fired. The squirrel dropped straight onto the road. I pulled back into the shadows and waited for something to happen, sure that someone must have heard the shot or seen the squirrel fall. But the sound that was so loud to me probably seemed to our neighbours no more than the bang of a cupboard slammed shut. After a while I sneaked a glance into the street. The squirrel hadn't moved. It looked like a scarf someone had dropped.

When my mother got home from work I told her there was a dead squirrel in the street. She took a cellophane bag off a loaf of bread and we went outside to where the squirrel lay. 'Poor little thing,' she said. She stuck her hand in the wrapper and picked up the squirrel, then pulled the bag inside-out away from her hand. We buried it behind our building under a cross made of popsicle sticks, and I blubbered the whole time.

I blubbered again in bed that night. At last I got out of bed and knelt down and did an imitation of somebody praying, and then I did an imitation of somebody receiving divine reassurance and inspiration. I stopped crying. I smiled to myself and forced a feeling of warmth into my chest. Then I climbed back in bed and looked up at the ceiling with a blissful expression until I went to sleep.

For several days I stayed away from the apartment at times when I knew I'd be alone there. I resumed my old patrol around the city or fooled around with my Mormon friends. Though I avoided the apartment, I could not get rid of the idea that sooner or later I would get the rifle out again. All my images of myself as I wished to be were images of myself armed. Because I did not know who I was, any image of myself, no matter how grotesque, had power over me. This much I understand now. But the man can give no help to the boy, not in this matter nor in those that follow. The boy moves always out of reach.

One afternoon I walked a friend of mine to his house. After he went inside I sat on his steps for a while, then got to my feet and started towards home, walking fast. The apartment was empty. I took the rifle out and cleaned it. Put it back. Ate a sandwich. Took the rifle out again. Though I did not load it I turned the lights off and pulled down the shades and assumed my position on the couch.

I stayed away for several days after that. Then I came back again. For an hour or so I aimed at people passing by. Again I teased myself by leaving the rifle unloaded, snapping the hammer on air, trying my own patience like a loose tooth. I had just followed a car out of sight when another car turned the corner at the bottom of the hill. I zeroed in on it, then lowered the rifle. I don't know whether I had ever seen this exact car before but it was of a type and color—big, plain, blue—usually driven only by government workers and nuns. You could tell if it was nuns by the way their headgear filled the windows and by the way they drove, which was very slowly and anxiously. Even from a distance you could feel the tension radiating from a car full of nuns.

The car crept up the hill. It moved even slower as it approached my building, and then it stopped. The front door on the passenger side opened and Sister James got out. I drew back from the window. When I looked out again, the car was still there but Sister James was not. I knew that the apartment door was locked—I always locked it when I took the rifle out—but I went over and double-checked it anyway. I heard her coming up the steps. She was whistling. She stopped outside the door and knocked. It was an imperative knock. She continued to whistle as she waited. She knocked again.

I stayed where I was, still and silent, rifle in hand, afraid that Sister James would somehow pass through the locked door and discover me. What would she think? What would she make of the rifle, the fur hat, the uniform, the darkened room? What would she make of me? I feared her disapproval, but even more than that I feared her incomprehension, even her amusement, at what she could not possibly understand. I didn't understand it myself. Being so close to so much robust identity made me feel the poverty of my own, the ludicrous aspect of my costume and props. I didn't want to let her in. At the same time, strangely, I did.

After a few moments of this an envelope slid under the door and I heard Sister James going back down the steps. I went to the window. I saw her bend low to enter the car, lifting her habit with one hand and reaching inside with the other. She arranged herself on the seat, closed the door, and the car started slowly up the hill. I never saw her again.

The envelope was addressed to Mrs Wolff. I tore it open and read the note. Sister James wanted my mother to call her. I burned the envelope and note in the sink and washed the ashes down the drain.

Roy was tying flies at the kitchen table. I was drinking a Pepsi and watching him. He bent close to his work, grunting with concentration. He said, in an offhand way, 'What do you think about a little brother?'

'A little brother?'

He nodded. 'Me and your mom've been thinking about starting a family.'

I didn't like this idea at all; in fact it froze me solid.

He looked up from the vise. 'We're already pretty much of a family when you think about it,' he said.

I said I guessed we were.

'We have a lot of fun.' He looked down at the vise again. 'A lot of fun. We're thinking about it,' he said. 'Nothing like a little guy around the house. You could teach him things. You could teach him to shoot.'

I nodded.

'That's what we were thinking too,' he said. 'I don't know about names, though. What do you think of Bill as a name?'

I said I liked it.

'Bill,' Roy said. 'Bill. Bill.' He turned silent again, staring down at the fly in the vise, hands on the table. I finished off my Pepsi and went outside.

While my mother and I ate breakfast the next morning Roy carried fishing gear and camping equipment out to the Jeep. He was lashing down something in back when I left for school. I yelled, 'Good luck!' and he waved at me, and I never saw him again either. My mother was in the apartment when I got home that day, folding clothes into a suitcase that lay open on her bed. Two other suitcases were already packed full. She was singing to herself. Her color was high, her movements quick and sure, everything about her flushed with gaiety. I knew we were on our way the moment I heard her voice, even before I saw the suitcases.

She asked me why I wasn't at archery. There was no suspicion behind the question.

'They cancelled it,' I told her.

'Great,' she said. 'Now I won't have to go looking for you. Why don't you check your room and make sure I've got everything?'

'We going somewhere?'

'Yes.' She smoothed out a dress. 'We sure are.'

'Where?'

She laughed. 'I don't know. Any suggestions?'

'Phoenix,' I said immediately.

She didn't ask why. She hung the dress in a garment bag and said, 'That's a real coincidence, because I was thinking about Phoenix myself. I even got the Phoenix paper. They have lots of opportunities there. Seattle too. What do you think about Seattle?'

I sat down on the bed. It was starting to take hold of me too, the giddiness of flight. My knees shook and I felt myself grin. Everything was racing. I said, 'What about Roy?'

She kept on packing. 'What about him?'

'I don't know. Is he coming too?'

'Not if I can help it, he isn't.' She said she hoped that was OK with me.

I didn't answer. I was afraid of saying something she would remember if they got back together. But I was glad to be once more on the run and glad that I would have her to myself again.

'I know you two are close,' she said.

'Not that close,' I said.

She said there wasn't time to explain everything now, but later on she would. She was trying to sound serious but she kept grinning back at me. She was close to laughing, and so was I.

'Better check your room,' my mother said again.

'When are we leaving?'

'Right away. As soon as we can.'

I ate a bowl of soup while my mother finished packing. She carried the suitcases into the front hall and then walked down to the corner to call a cab. That was when I remembered the rifle. I went to the closet and saw it there with Roy's things, his boots and jackets and ammo boxes. I carried the rifle to the living-room and waited for my mother to come back.

'That thing stays,' she said when she saw it.

'It's mine,' I said.

'Don't make a scene,' she told me. 'I've had enough of those things. I'm sick of them. Now put it back.'

'It's mine,' I repeated. 'He gave it to me.'

'No. I'm sick of guns.'

'Mom, it's *mine*.'

She looked out the window. 'No. We don't have room for it.'

This was a mistake. She had put the argument in practical terms and now it would be impossible for her to argue from principle again. 'Look,' I said, 'there's room. See, I can break it down.' And before she could stop me I had unscrewed the locking bolt and pulled the rifle apart. I dragged one of the suitcases back into the living-room and unzipped it and slid the two halves of the rifle in between the clothes. 'See?' I said. 'There's room.'

She had been watching me with her arms crossed, her lips pressed tightly together. She turned to the window again. 'Keep it then,' she said. 'If it means that much to you.'

It was raining when our cab pulled up. The cabby honked and my mother started wrestling one of the suitcases down the steps. The cabby saw her and got out to help, a big man in a fancy western shirt that got soaked in the drizzle. He went back for the other two bags while we waited in the cab. My mother kidded him about how wet he was and he kidded her back, looking in the rear-view mirror constantly as if to make sure she was still there. As we approached the Greyhound station he stopped joking and began to quiz her in a low, hurried voice, asking one question after another, and when I got out of the cab he pulled the door shut behind me, leaving the two of them alone inside. Through the water streaming down the window I could see him talking, talking, and my mother smiling and shaking her head. Then they both got out and he took our bags from the truck. 'You're sure now?' he said to her. She nodded. When she tried to pay him he said that her money was no good, not to him it wasn't, but she held it out again and he took it.

My mother broke out laughing after he drove away. 'Of all things,' she said. She kept laughing to herself as we hauled the bags inside, where she settled me on a bench and went to the ticket window. The station was empty except for a family of Indians. All of them, even the children, looked straight ahead and said nothing. A few minutes later my mother came back with our tickets. The Phoenix bus had left already and the next one didn't come through until late that night, but we were in luck—there was a bus leaving for Portland in a couple of hours, and from there we could make an easy connection to Seattle. I tried to conceal my disappointment but my mother saw it and bought me off with a handful of change. I played the pinball machines for a while and then stocked up on candy bars for the trip, Milk Duds and Sugar Babies and Idaho Spuds, most of which were already curdling in my stomach when at dusk we boarded our bus and stood in the dazed regard of the other passengers. We hesitated for a moment as if we might get off. Then my mother took my hand and we made our way down the aisle, nodding to anyone who looked at us, smiling to show we meant well.

Peter Carey
A Letter to our Son

Before I have finished writing this, the story of how you were born, I will be forty-four years old and the events and feelings which make up the story will be at least eight months old. You are lying in the next room in a cotton jump-suit. You have five teeth. You cannot walk. You do not seem interested in crawling. You are sound asleep.

I have put off writing this so long that, now the time is here, I do not want to write it. I cannot think. Laziness. Wooden shutters over the memory. Nothing comes, no pictures, no feelings, but the architecture of the hospital at Camperdown.

You were born in the King George V Hospital in Missenden Road, Camperdown, a building that won an award for its architecture. It was opened during the Second World War, but its post-Bauhaus modern style has its roots in that time before the First World War, with an optimism about the technological future that we may never have again.

I liked this building. I liked its smooth, rounded, shiny corners. I liked its wide stairs, I liked the huge sash-windows, even the big blue-and-white checked tiles: when I remember this building there is sunshine splashed across those tiles, but there were times when it seemed that other memories might triumph and it would be remembered for the harshness of its neon lights and emptiness of the corridors.

A week before you were born, I sat with your mother in a four-bed ward on the eleventh floor of this building. In this ward she received blood transfusions from plum-red plastic bags suspended on rickety stainless steel stands. The blood did not always flow smoothly. The bags had to be fiddled with, the stand had to be raised, lowered, have its drip-rate increased, decreased, inspected by the sister who had been a political prisoner in Chile, by the sister from the Solomon Islands, by others I don't remember. The blood entered your mother through a needle in her forearm. When the vein collapsed, a new one had to be found. This was caused by a kind of bruising called 'tissuing'. We soon knew all about tissuing. It made her arm hurt like hell.

She was bright-eyed and animated as always, but her lips had a slight blue tinge and her skin had a tight, translucent quality.

She was in this room on the west because her blood appeared

to be dying. Some thought the blood was killing itself. This is what we all feared, none more than me, for when I heard her blood-count was so low, the first thing I thought (stop that thought, cut it off, bury it) was cancer.

This did not necessarily have a lot to do with Alison, but with me, and how I had grown up, with a mother who was preoccupied with cancer and who, going into surgery for suspected breast cancer, begged the doctor to 'cut them both off'. When my mother's friend Enid Tanner boasted of her hard stomach muscles, my mother envisaged a growth. When her father complained of a sore elbow, my mother threatened the old man: 'All right, we'll take you up to Doctor Campbell and she'll cut it off.' When I was ten, my mother's brother got cancer and they cut his leg off right up near the hip and took photographs of him, naked, one-legged, to show other doctors the success of the operation.

When I heard your mother's blood-count was low, I was my mother's son. I thought: cancer.

I remembered what Alison had told me of that great tragedy of her grandparents' life, how their son (her uncle) had leukaemia, how her grandfather then bought him the car (a Ford Prefect? a Morris Minor?) he had hitherto refused him, how the dying boy had driven for miles and miles, hours and hours while his cells attacked each other.

I tried to stop this thought, to cut it off. It grew again, like a thistle whose root has not been removed and must grow again, every time, stronger and stronger.

The best haematological unit in Australia was on hand to deal with the problem. They worked in the hospital across the road, the Royal Prince Alfred. They were friendly and efficient. They were not at all like I had imagined big hospital specialists to be. They took blood samples, but the blood did not tell them enough. They returned to take marrow from your mother's bones. They brought a big needle with them that would give you the horrors if you could see the size of it.

The doctor's speciality was leukaemia, but he said to us: 'We don't think it's anything really nasty.' Thus 'nasty' became a code for cancer.

They diagnosed megnoblastic anaemia which, although we did

not realize it, is the condition of the blood and not the disease itself.

Walking back through the streets in Shimbashi in Tokyo, your mother once told me that a fortune-teller had told her she would die young. It was for this reason—or so I remembered—that she took such care of her health. At the time she told me this, we had not known each other very long. It was July. We had fallen in love in May. We were still stumbling over each other's feelings in the dark. I took this secret of your mother's lightly, not thinking about the weight it must carry, what it might mean to talk about it. I hurt her; we fought, in the street by the Shimbashi railway station, in a street with shop windows advertising cosmetic surgery, in the Dai-Ichi Hotel in the Ginza district of Tokyo, Japan.

When they took the bone marrow from your mother's spine, I held her hand. The needle had a cruel diameter, was less a needle than an instrument for removing a plug. She was very brave. Her wrists seemed too thin, her skin too white and shiny, her eyes too big and bright. She held my hand because of pain. I held hers because I loved her, because I could not think of living if I did not have her. I thought of what she had told me in Tokyo. I wished there was a God I could pray to.

I flew to Canberra on 7 May 1984. It was my forty-first birthday. I had injured my back and should have been lying flat on a board. I had come from a life with a woman which had reached, for both of us, a state of chronic unhappiness. I will tell you the truth: I was on that aeroplane to Canberra because I hoped I might fall in love. This made me a dangerous person.

There was a playwrights' conference in Canberra. I hoped there would be a woman there who would love me as I would love her. This was a fantasy I had had before, getting on aeroplanes to foreign cities, riding in taxis towards hotels in Melbourne, in Adelaide, in Brisbane. I do not mean that I was thinking about sex, or an affair, but that I was looking for someone to spend my life with. Also—and I swear I have not invented this after the fact—I had a vision of your mother's neck.

I hardly knew her. I met her once at a dinner when I hardly noticed her. I met her a second time when I saw, in a meeting room, the back of her neck. We spoke that time, but I was argumentative and I did not think of her in what I can only call 'that way'.

And yet as the aeroplane came down to land in Canberra, I saw your mother's neck, and thought: maybe Alison Summers will be there. She was the dramaturge at the Nimrod Theatre. It was a playwrights' conference. She should be there.

And she was. And we fell in love. And we stayed up till four in the morning every morning talking. And there were other men, everywhere, in love with her. I didn't know about the other men. I knew only that I was in love as I had not been since I was eighteen years old. I wanted to marry Alison Summers, and at the end of the first night we had been out together when I walked her to the door of her room, and we had, for the first time, ever so lightly, kissed on the lips—and also, I must tell you, for it was delectable and wonderful, I kissed your mother on her long, beautiful neck—and when we had kissed and patted the air between us and said 'all right' a number of times, and I had walked back to my room where I had, because of my back injury, a thin mattress lying flat on the floor, and when I was in this bed, I said, aloud, to the empty room: 'I am going to live with Alison.'

And I went to sleep so happy I must have been smiling.

She did not know what I told the room. And it was three or four days before I could see her again, three or four days before we could go out together, spend time alone, and I could tell her what I thought.

I had come to Canberra wanting to fall in love. Now I was in love. Who was I in love with? I hardly knew, and yet I knew exactly. I did not even realize how beautiful she was. I found that out later. At the beginning I recognized something more potent than beauty: it was a force, a life, an energy. She had such life in her face, in her eyes—those eyes which you inherited—most of all. It was this I loved, this which I recognized so that I could say—having kissed her so lightly—I will live with Alison. And know that I was right.

It was a conference. We were behaving like men and women do at conferences, having affairs. We would not be so sleazy. After four nights staying up talking till four a.m. we had still not made love. I would creep back to my room, to my mattress on the floor. We talked about everything. Your mother liked me, but I cannot tell you how long it took her to fall in love with me. But I know we were discussing marriages and babies when we had not even been to bed together. That came early one morning when I returned to her room after three hours' sleep. We had not planned to make love there at the conference but there we were, lying on the bed, kissing, and then we were making love, and you were not conceived then, of course, and yet from that time we never ceased thinking of you and when, later in Sydney, we had to learn to adjust to each other's needs, and when we argued, which we did often then, it was you more than anything that kept us together. We wanted you so badly. We loved you before we saw you. We loved you as we made you, in bed in another room, at Lovett Bay.

When your mother came to the eleventh floor of the King George V Hospital, you were almost ready to be born. Every day the sisters came and smeared jelly on your mother's tight, bulging stomach and then stuck a flat little octopus-type sucker to it and listened to the noises you made.

You sounded like soldiers marching on a bridge.

You sounded like short-wave radio.

You sounded like the inside of the sea.

We did not know if you were a boy or a girl, but we called you Sam anyway. When you kicked or turned we said, 'Sam's doing his exercises.' We said silly things.

When we heard how low Alison's blood-count was, I phoned the obstetrician to see if you were OK. She said there was no need to worry. She said you had your own blood-supply. She said that as long as the mother's count was above six there was no need to worry.

You mother's count was 6.2. This was very close. I kept worrying that you had been hurt in some way. I could not share this worry for to share it would only be to make it worse. Also I recognize that I have made a whole career out of making my anxieties get up and walk around, not only in my own mind, but in the minds of readers. I went to see a naturopath once. We talked about negative emotions—fear and anger. I said to him, 'But I *use* my anger and my fear.' I talked about these emotions as if they were chisels and hammers.

This alarmed him considerably.

Your mother is not like this. When the haematologists saw how she looked, they said: 'Our feeling is that you don't have anything nasty.' They topped her up with blood until her count was twelve and although they had not located the source of her anaemia, they sent her home.

A few days later her count was down to just over six.

It seemed as if there was a silent civil war inside her veins and arteries. The number of casualties was appalling.

I think we both got frightened then. I remember coming home to Louisa Road. I remember worrying that I would cry. I remember embracing your mother—and you too, for you were a great bulge between us. I must not cry. I must support her.

I made a meal. It was salade niçoise. The electric lights, in memory, were all ten watts, sapped by misery. I could barely eat. I think we may have watched a funny film on videotape. We repacked the bag that had been unpacked so short a time before. It now seemed likely that your birth was to be induced. If your mother was sick she could not be looked after properly with you inside her. She would be given one more blood transfusion, and then the induction would begin. And that is how your birthday would be on September thirteenth.

Two nights before your birthday I sat with Alison in the four-bed ward, the one facing east, towards Missenden Road. The curtains were drawn around us. I sat on the bed and held her hand. The blood continued its slow viscous drip from the plum-red bag along the clear plastic tube and into her arm. The obstetrician was with us. She stood at the head of the bed, a kind, intelligent woman in her early thirties. We talked about Alison's blood. We asked her what she thought this mystery could be. Really what we wanted was to be told that everything was OK. There was a look on Alison's face when she asked. I cannot describe it, but it was not a face seeking medical 'facts'.

The obstetrician went through all the things that were not wrong with your mother's blood. She did not have a vitamin B deficiency. She did not have a folic acid deficiency. There was no iron deficiency. She did not have any of the common (and easily fixable) anaemias of pregnancy. So what could it be? we asked, really only wishing to be assured it was nothing 'nasty'.

'Well,' said the obstetrician, 'at this stage you cannot rule out cancer.'

I watched your mother's face. Nothing in her expression showed what she must feel. There was a slight colouring of her cheeks. She nodded. She asked a question or two. She held my hand, but there was no tight squeezing.

The obstetrician asked Alison if she was going to be 'all right'. Alison said she would be 'all right'. But when the obstetrician left she left the curtains drawn.

The obstetrician's statement was not of course categorical and not everyone who has cancer dies, but Alison was, at that instant, confronting the thing that we fear most. When the doctor said those words, it was like a dream or a nightmare. I heard them said. And yet they were not said. They could not be said. And when we hugged each other—when the doctor had gone—we pressed our bodies together as we always had before, and if there were tears on our cheeks, there had been tears on our cheeks before. I kissed your mother's eyes. Her hair was wet with her tears. I smoothed her hair on her forehead. My own eyes were swimming. She said: 'All right, how are we going to get through all this?'

Now you know her, you know how much like her that is. She is not going to be a victim of anything.

'We'll decide it's going to be OK,' she said, 'that's all.'

And we dried our eyes.

But that night, when she was alone in her bed, waiting for the sleeping pill to work, she thought: If I die, I'll at least have made this little baby.

When I left your mother I appeared dry-eyed and positive, but my disguise was a frail shell of a thing and it cracked on the stairs and my grief and rage came spilling out in gulps. The halls of the hospital gleamed with polish and vinyl and fluorescent light. The flower-seller on the ground floor had locked up his shop. The foyer was empty. The whisker-shadowed man in admissions was watching television. In Missenden Road two boys in jeans and sand-shoes conducted separate conversations in separate phone booths. Death was not touching them. They turned their backs to each other. One of them—a red-head with a tattoo on his forearm—laughed.

In Missenden Road there were taxis NOT FOR HIRE speeding towards other destinations.

In Missenden Road the bright white lights above the zebra crossings became a luminous sea inside my eyes. Car lights turned into necklaces and ribbons. I was crying, thinking it is not for me to cry: crying is a poison, a negative force; everything will be all right; but I was weeping as if huge balloons of air had to be released from inside my guts. I walked normally. My grief was invisible. A man rushed past me, carrying roses wrapped in cellophane. I got into my car. The floor was littered with car-park tickets from all the previous days of blood transfusions, tests, test results, admission etc. I drove out of the car-park. I talked aloud.

I told the night I loved Alison Summers. I love you, I love you, you will not die. There were red lights at the Parramatta Road. I sat there, howling, unroadworthy. I love you.

The day after tomorrow there will be a baby. Will the baby have a mother? What would we do if we knew Alison was dying? What would we do so Sam would know his mother? Would we make a videotape? Would we hire a camera? Would we set it up and act for you? Would we talk to you with smiling faces, showing you how we were together, how we loved each other? How could we? How could we think of these things?

I was a prisoner in a nightmare driving down Ross Street in Glebe. I passed the Afrikan restaurant where your mother and I ate after first coming to live in Balmain.

All my life I have waited for this woman. This cannot happen.

I thought: Why would it *not* happen? Every day people are tortured, killed, bombed. Every day babies starve. Every day there is pain and grief, enough to make you howl to the moon forever. Why should we be exempt, I thought, from the pain of life?

What would I do with a baby? How would I look after it? Day after day, minute after minute, by myself. I would be a sad man, forever, marked by the loss of this woman. I would love the baby. I would care for it. I would see, in its features, every day, the face of the woman I had loved more than any other.

When I think of this time, it seems as if it's two in the morning, but it was not. It was ten o'clock at night. I drove home through a landscape of grotesque imaginings.

The house was empty and echoing.

In the nursery everything was waiting for you, all the things we had got for 'the baby'. We had read so many books about babies, been to classes where we learned about how babies are born, but we still did not understand the purpose of all the little clothes we had folded in the drawers. We did not know which was a swaddle and which was a sheet. We could not have selected the clothes to dress you in.

I drank coffee. I drank wine. I set out to telephone Kathy Lette, Alison's best friend, so she would have this 'news' before she spoke to your mother the next day. I say 'set out' because each time I began to dial, I thought: I am not going to do this properly. I hung up. I did deep breathing. I calmed myself. I telephoned. Kim Williams, Kathy's husband, answered and said Kathy was not home yet. I thought: She must know. I told Kim, and as I told him the weeping came with it. I could hear myself. I could imagine Kim listening to me. I would sound frightening, grotesque, and less in control than I was. When I had finished frightening him, I went to bed and slept.

I do not remember the next day, only that we were bright and determined. Kathy hugged Alison and wept. I hugged Kathy and wept. There were isolated incidents. We were 'handling it'. And, besides, you were coming on the next day. You were life, getting stronger and stronger.

I had practical things to worry about. For instance: the bag. The bag was to hold all the things for the labour ward. There was a list for the contents of the bag and these contents were all purchased and ready, but still I must bring them to the hospital early the next morning. I checked the bag. I placed things where I would not forget them. You wouldn't believe the things we had. We had a cassette-player and a tape with soothing music. We had rosemary and lavender oil so I could massage your mother and relax her between contractions. I had a thermos to fill with blocks of frozen orange juice. There were special cold packs to relieve the pain of a backache labour. There were paper pants—your arrival, after all, was not to happen without a great deal of mess. There were socks, because your mother's feet would almost certainly get very cold. I packed all these things, and there was something in the process of this packing which helped overcome my fears and made me concentrate on you, our little baby, already so loved although we did not know your face, had seen no more of you than the ghostly blue image thrown up by the ultrasound in the midst of whose shifting perspectives we had seen your little hand move. ('He waved to us.')

On the morning of the day of your birth I woke early. It was only just light. I had notes stuck on the fridge and laid out on the table. I made coffee and poured it into a thermos. I made the bagel sandwiches your mother and I had planned months before—my lunch. I filled the bagels with a fiery Polish sausage and cheese and gherkins. For your mother, I filled a spray-bottle with Evian water.

It was a Saturday morning and bright and sunny and I knew you would be born but I did not know what it would be like. I drove along Ross Street in Glebe ignorant of the important things I would know that night. I wore grey stretchy trousers and a black shirt which would later be marked by the white juices of your birth. I was excited, but less than you might imagine. I parked at the hospital as I had parked on all those other occasions. I carried the bags up to the eleventh floor. They were heavy.

Alison was in her bed. She looked calm and beautiful. When we kissed, her lips were soft and tender. She said: 'This time tomorrow we'll have a little baby.'

In our conversation, we used the diminutive a lot. You were always spoken of as 'little', as indeed you must really have been, but we would say 'little' hand, 'little' feet, 'little' baby, and thus evoked all our powerful feelings about you.

This term ('little') is so loaded that writers are wary of using it. It is cute, sentimental, 'easy'. All of sentient life seems programmed to respond to 'little'. If you watch grown dogs with a pup, a pup they have never seen, they are immediately patient and gentle, even

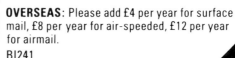

No postage
necessary
if posted
in the UK

Granta
FREEPOST
Cambridge
CB1 1BR

No postage
necessary
if posted
in the UK

Granta
FREEPOST
Cambridge
CB1 1BR

solicitous, with it. If you had watched your mother and father holding up a tiny terry-towelling jump-suit in a department store, you would have seen their faces change as they celebrated your 'littleness' while, at the same time, making fun of their own responses—they were aware of acting in a way they would have previously thought of as saccharine.

And yet we were not aware of the torrents of emotion your 'littleness' would unleash in us, and by the end of September thirteenth we would think it was nothing other than the meaning of life itself.

When I arrived at the hospital with the heavy bags of cassette-players and rosemary oil, I saw a dark-bearded, neat man in a suit sitting out by the landing. This was the hypnotherapist who had arrived to help you come into the world. He was serious, impatient, eager to start. He wanted to start in the pathology ward, but in the end he helped carry the cassette-player, thermoses, sandwiches, massage oil, sponges, paper pants, apple juice, frozen orange blocks, rolling pin, cold packs, and even water down to the labour ward where—on a stainless steel stand eight feet high—the sisters were already hanging the bag of Oxytocin which would ensure this day was your birthday.

It was a pretty room, by the taste of the time. As I write it is still that time, and I still think it pretty. All the surfaces were hospital surfaces—easy to clean—laminexes, vinyls, materials with a hard shininess, but with colours that were soft pinks and blues and an effect that was unexpectedly pleasant, even sophisticated.

The bed was one of those complicated stainless steel machines which seems so cold and impersonal until you realize all the clever things it can do. In the wall there were sockets with labels like 'Oxygen'. The cupboards were filled with paper-wrapped sterile 'objects'. There was, in short, a seriousness about the room, and when we plugged in the cassette-player we took care to make sure we were not using a socket that might be required for something more important.

The hypnotherapist left me to handle the unpacking of the bags. He explained his business to the obstetrician. She told him that eight hours would be a good, fast labour. The hypnotherapist said he and Alison were aiming for three. I don't know what the doctor thought, but I thought there was not a hope in hell.

When the Oxytocin drip had been put into my darling's arm, when the water-clear hormone was entering her veins, one drip every ten seconds (you could hear the machine click when a drip was released), when these pure chemical messages were being delivered to her body, the hypnotherapist attempted to send other messages of a less easily assayable quality.

I tell you the truth: I did not care for this hypnotherapist, this pushy, over-eager fellow taking up all this room in the labour ward. He sat on the right-hand side of the bed. I sat on the left. He made me feel useless. He said: 'You are going to have a good labour, a fast labour, a fast labour like the one you have already visualized.' Your mother's eyes were closed. She had such large, soft lids, such tender and vulnerable coverings of skin. Inside the pink light of the womb, your eyelids were the same. Did you hear the messages your mother was sending to her body and to you? The hypnotherapist said: 'After just three hours you are going to deliver a baby, a good, strong, healthy baby. It will be an easy birth, an effortless birth. It will last three hours and you will not tear.' On the door the sisters had tacked a sign reading: QUIET PLEASE. HYPNOTHERAPY IN PROGRESS. 'You are going to be so relaxed, and in a moment you are going to be even more relaxed, more relaxed than you have ever been before. You are feeling yourself going deeper and deeper and when you come to you will be in a state of waking hypnosis and you will respond to the trigger-words Peter will give you during your labour, words which will make you, once again, so relaxed.'

My trigger-words were to be 'Breathe' and 'Relax'.

The hypnotherapist gave me his phone number and asked me to call when you were born. But for the moment you had not felt the effects of the Oxytocin on your world and you could not yet have suspected the adventures the day would have in store for you.

You still sounded like the ocean, like soldiers marching across a bridge, like short-wave radio.

On Tuesday nights through the previous winter we had gone to classes in a building where the lifts were always sticking. We had walked up the stairs to a room where pregnant women and their partners had rehearsed birth with dolls, had watched hours of videotapes of exhausted women in labour. We had practised all the different sorts of breathing. We had learned of the different positions for giving birth: the squat, the supported squat, the squat supported by a seated partner. We knew the positions for first and second stage, for a backache labour, and so on, and so on. We learned birth was a complicated, exhausting and difficult process. We worried we would forget how to breathe. And yet now the time was here we both felt confident, even though nothing would be like it had been in the birth classes. Your mother was connected to the Oxytocin drip which meant she could not get up and walk around. It meant it was difficult for her to 'belly dance' or do most of the things we had spent so many evenings learning about.

In the classes they tell you that the contractions will start far apart, that you should go to hospital only when they are ten minutes apart: short bursts of pain, but long rests in between. During this period your mother could expect to walk around, to listen to music, to enjoy a massage. However, your birth was not to be like this. This was not because of you. It was because of the Oxytocin. It had a fast, intense effect, like a double Scotch when you're expecting a beer. There were not to be any ten-minute rests, and from the time the labour started it was, almost immediately, fast and furious, with a one-minute contraction followed by no more than two minutes of rest.

If there had been time to be frightened, I think I would have been frightened. Your mother was in the grip of pains she could not escape from. She squatted on a bean bag. It was as if her insides were all tangled, and tugged in a battle to the death. Blood ran from her. Fluid like egg-white. I did not know what anything was. I was a man who had wandered onto a battlefield. The blood was bright with oxygen. I wiped your mother's brow. She panted. *Huh-huh-huh-huh.* I ministered to her with sponge and water. I could not take her pain for her. I could do nothing but measure the duration of the pain. I had a little red stop-watch you will one day find abandoned in a dusty drawer. (Later your mother asked me what I had felt during labour. I thought only: I must count the seconds of the contraction; I must help Alison breathe, now, now, now; I must get that sponge—there is time to make the water in the sponge cool—

now I can remove that bowl and cover it. Perhaps I can reach the bottle of Evian water. God, I'm so *thirsty*. What did I think during the labour? I thought: When this contraction is over I will get to that Evian bottle.)

Somewhere in the middle of this, in these three hours in this room whose only view was a blank screen of frosted glass, I helped your mother climb onto the bed. She was on all fours. In this position she could reach the gas mask. It was nitrous oxide, laughing gas. It did not stop the pain, but it made it less important. For the gas to work your mother had to anticipate the contraction, breathing in gas before it arrived. The sister came and showed me how I could feel the contraction coming with my hand. But I couldn't. We used the stop-watch, but the contractions were not regularly spaced, and sometimes we anticipated them and sometimes not. When we did not get it right, your mother took the full brunt of the pain. She had her face close to the mattress. I sat on the chair beside. My face was close to hers. I held the watch where she could see it. I held her wrist. I can still see the red of her face, the wideness of her eyes as they bulged at the enormous *size* of the pains that racked her.

Sisters came and went. They had to see how wide the cervix was. At first it was only two centimetres, not nearly enough room for you to come out. An hour later they announced it was four centimetres. It had to get to nine centimetres before we could even think of you being born. There had to be room for your head (which we had been told was big—well, we were told wrong, weren't we?) and your shoulders to slip through. It felt to your mother that this labour would go on for eight or twelve or twenty hours. That she should endure this intensity of pain for this time was unthinkable. It was like running a hundred-metre race which was stretching to ten miles. She wanted an epidural—a pain blocker.

But when the sister heard this she said: 'Oh do try to hang on. You're doing *so* well.'

I went to the sister, like a shop steward.

I said: 'My wife wants an epidural, so can you please arrange it?'

The sister agreed to fetch the anaesthetist, but there was

between us—I admit it now—a silent conspiracy: for although I had pressed the point and she had agreed it was your mother's right, we both believed (I, for my part, on her advice) that if your mother could endure a little longer she could have the birth she wanted—without an epidural.

The anaesthetist came and went. The pain was at its worst. A midwife came and inspected your mother. She said: 'Ten centimetres.'

She said: 'Your baby is about to be born.'

We kissed, your mother and I. We kissed with soft, passionate lips as we did the day we lay on a bed at Lovett Bay and conceived you. That day the grass outside the window was a brilliant green beneath the vibrant petals of fallen jacaranda.

Outside the penumbra of our consciousness trolleys were wheeled. Sterile bags were cut open. The contractions did not stop, of course.

The obstetrician had not arrived. She was in a car, driving fast towards the hospital.

I heard a midwife say: 'Who can deliver in this position?' (It was still unusual, as I learned at that instant, for women to deliver their babies on all fours.)

Someone left the room. Someone entered. Your mother was pressing the gas mask so hard against her face it was making deep indentations on her skin. Her eyes bulged huge.

Someone said: 'Well get her, otherwise I'll have to deliver it myself.'

The door opened. Bushfire came in.

Bushfire was aboriginal. She was about fifty years old. She was compact and taciturn like a farmer. She had a face that folded in on itself and let out its feelings slowly, selectively. It was a face to trust, and trust especially at this moment when I looked up to see Bushfire coming through the door in a green gown. She came in a rush, her hands out to have gloves put on.

There was another contraction. I heard the latex snap around Bushfire's wrists. She said: 'There it is. I can see your baby's head.' It was you. The tip of you, the top of you. You were a new country, a planet, a star seen for the first time. I was not looking at Bushfire.

I was looking at your mother. She was all alight with love and pain.

'Push,' said Bushfire.

Your mother pushed. It was you she was pushing, you that put that look of luminous love on her face, you that made the veins on her forehead bulge and her skin go red.

Then—it seems such a short time later—Bushfire said: 'Your baby's head is born.'

And then, so quickly in retrospect, but one can no more recall it accurately than one can recall exactly how one made love on a bed when the jacaranda petals were lying like jewels on the grass outside. Soon. Soon we heard you. Soon you slipped out of your mother. Soon you came slithering out not having hurt her, not even having grazed her. You slipped out, as slippery as a little fish, and we heard you cry. Your cry was so much lighter and thinner than I might have expected. I do not mean that it was weak or frail, but that your first cry had a timbre unlike anything I had expected. The joy we felt. Your mother and I kissed again, at that moment.

'My little baby,' she said. We were crying with happiness. 'My little baby.'

I turned to look. I saw you. Skin. Blue-white, shiny-wet.

I said: 'It's a boy.'

'Look at me,' your mother said, meaning: stay with me, be with me, the pain is not over yet, do not leave me now. I turned to her. I kissed her. I was crying, just crying with happiness that you were there.

The room you were born in was quiet, not full of noise and clattering. This is how we wanted it for you. So you could come into the world gently and that you should—as you were now—be put onto your mother's stomach. They wrapped you up. I said: 'Couldn't he feel his mother's skin?' They unwrapped you so you could have your skin against hers.

And there you were. It was you. You had a face, the face we had never known. You were so calm. You did not cry or fret. You had big eyes like your mother's. And yet when I looked at you first I saw not your mother and me, but your two grandfathers, your mother's father, my father; and, as my father, whom I loved a great deal, had died the year before, I was moved to see that here, in you, he was alive.

Look at the photographs in the album that we took at this time. Look at your mother and how alive she is, how clear her eyes are, how all the red pain has just slipped off her face and left the unmistakable visage of a young woman in love.

We bathed you (I don't know whether this was before or after) in warm water and you accepted this gravely, swimming instinctively.

I held you (I think this must be before), and you were warm and slippery. You had not been bathed when I held you. The obstetrician gave you to me so she could examine your mother. She said: 'Here.'

I held you against me. I knew then that your mother would not die. I thought: 'It's fine, it's all right.' I held you against my breast. You smelled of love-making.

GRANTA

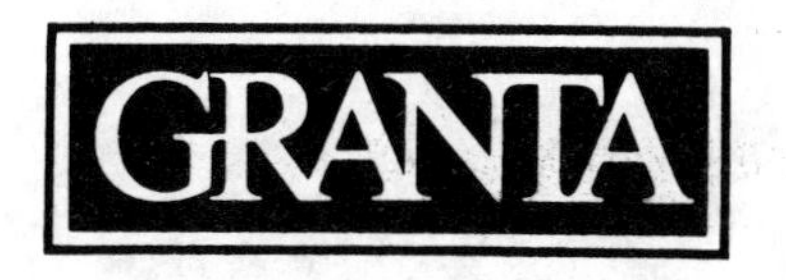

James Fenton
Kwangju and After

Photo: Philip J Griffiths (Magnum)

In 1980 I had, for personal reasons, to revisit Thailand. I hadn't wanted to. Indeed I had often vowed that I would never go back to the Far East. Also, I was absolutely determined never again to work as a foreign correspondent.

But there I was, staying at the Trocadero with several other journalists, and the conversation turned to South Korea. It seemed that the students had armed themselves and had managed to throw the army out of a city called Kwangju—an extraordinary event, an improbability, armed insurrection in one of the most authoritarian countries in the world.

Before long, the journalists' luggage began to appear in the hotel lobby, and anxious trips were made to travel agents. I watched all this with superior detachment. As far as I was concerned, they could keep South Korea, that terrifying place. It had one of the world's most efficient secret services. It crushed dissent at home and pursued it ruthlessly abroad. Its power struggles were bloody. Its soldiers had been the most detested foreign troops in Vietnam. It was a place to avoid.

There was no question of my being sent there. I was a theatre critic, on holiday. As I bade farewell to my departing colleagues, I congratulated myself on my escape.

Then, passing the reception desk, I noticed I had a cable. 'Sorry to interrupt your holiday, James, but would you mind going to South Korea . . .?' Immediately I found myself thinking: South Korea! Of *course*, I'd *love* to go to South Korea. Just to *see* for myself what it's like. Having *heard* so much about it. Sounds *fascinating*.

2

I arrived on a Sunday evening, which meant that I had five days or so before writing my piece. Somehow in that time I was going to have to acquaint myself with the broader issues in Korean politics. If I spent this time hanging around the road-blocks, trying to get into Kwangju, I might learn and see nothing. I knew nobody in Korea and hadn't any idea what I was going to do.

When the hotel bellboy extracted from me the information that

I was a journalist, and when he immediately said, 'You must go to Kwangju tomorrow,' I became suspicious. I thought he was setting me up for some kind of trap. I paid him and proceeded to run a bath. Just as I was stepping in, the phone rang.

'Bellboy here!' A journalist from one of the agencies had just returned from Kwangju and was in the lobby. I must come down right away.

Quickly drying off the bath-foam suds, I pulled on my clothes and went down. The agency journalist was of Australian build, an intimidating figure in a Saigon safari suit. The tiny bellboy pointed him out and more or less ordered me to go and talk to him. The journalist was covered with the dust and sweat of the day. He didn't see why he should talk; nor could I. I did my best, before retreating in tongue-tied shame. And I had lost face with the bellboy. He couldn't see why I hadn't tried harder.

I retired to my room, took my clothes off and stepped into the bath. At precisely that moment, the phone rang again. It was the bellboy. A French photographer had just flown in and was looking for someone with whom to share a car to Kwangju; we would have to take a car, because there was no public transport; and we would need packed lunches from the hotel, because there was no food in Kwangju; the bellboy had already found us a driver and was negotiating on our behalf; could I please come down at once?

By now, I thought: Either this bellboy is a genius, or I am about to fall into some horrible trap laid by the Korean CIA. But what can I do? I was already beginning to panic about my article. Even the *bellboy* seemed to be panicking about my article: I would have to leave at four in the morning, he told me; I would have to sleep early—he'd thought of everything.

The French photographer, slim, dark, hungry and doomed, had just, he told me, flown over the North Pole to reach here, and the way he said it gave the impression that the polar route was something he had discovered, against all the odds, with a team of dogs. We made our arrangements and parted—I to my bath, which this time the bellboy allowed me to enjoy for five minutes, before announcing the return of several more journalists. By the end of the evening I had already met some people who had tried to get into Kwangju. Progress had been made. The bellboy watched me beadily as I pressed for the lift.

'Did you order the packed lunches?' he asked.

'I'm sorry, I didn't,' I said, feeling drained and incompetent.

'It's OK,' he said. '*I* did.'

3

In the dark, Etienne seemed to huddle for warmth against the rear seat of the car. 'I wish I was back in Paris,' he said, 'in bed,' and he paused before emphasizing 'with a woman in my arms.' He sounded as if he'd learned his French accent from a bad film whose lines kept coming back to him.

I'd seen Etienne before in Cambodia, and I wasn't entirely happy to be in his company. He gave the impression of a man forever travelling towards his death—a death which he was inviting you to mourn in advance. He was avid for nicotine and sympathy.

The motorway was eerily empty, and the countryside at dawn was extremely beautiful. I felt as if we were travelling down the *autostrada del sole*, but a mysterious power had changed the vineyards into paddy-fields. The agriculture was neat and intensive. Many of the fields were wrapped in polythene. The children went to school wearing cadet uniforms modelled after the Japanese style, which was in turn copied from Germany in the last century. Many of the houses had blue ceramic roofs. It was a cheerful sight.

Our driver seemed to be cast in the same mould as the hotel bellboy for he was completely unfazed by the road-blocks. We left the motorway and headed off into the hills in order to approach Kwangju from the flank. And even on these narrow roads there were check-points, but each time—how, I couldn't tell—the driver managed to get us through by talking, talking, talking. By now, the countryside seemed much poorer—it felt as if we were going back centuries—and most of the villagers were in traditional dress.

We came down out of the hills to a town with broad streets. This was Kwangju. Or at least the driver said it was. Etienne was dismayed. There were soldiers everywhere. We thought that the army must have come back in, and that the insurrection was over.

Then came a moment of intense drama. We suddenly realized

that the soldiers were not soldiers at all: these guys in uniforms and black, lobster-tail helmets were actually the students. Somehow or other we had crossed the lines.

The driver stopped. We left the car and walked a little way along a street. People hurried past us with averted faces. We stopped for a moment by a military truck, thinking that the slumped, helmeted figures in the cab were dead. But they were only sleeping. Then Etienne seemed to experience a rush of adrenalin. He shot off and I never saw him again.

I was very nervous. It takes a while, in any new country, to learn to read facial expressions and gestures. But here, barely able to guess who was who and what was what, I was completely disoriented and felt particularly unsafe. The driver could scarcely speak English, though he was very keen to help. People gathered around the car, and he asked them questions. An intense discussion followed, of which I was able to understand practically nothing, except the name of Chun Doo-hwan, continually repeated.

I walked towards the building which housed the regional administration, which had been taken over by very frightened-looking armed students. In front lay a row of sixteen open coffins, containing as yet unidentified victims of the earlier massacre. In all, that day, I saw eighty coffins, but people were already saying what has been rumoured since, that many, many more people had been killed. The military had, it seemed, run amok in the city. The students, in response, had raided the civil defence arsenals and, with the help of the people of the town, had forced the military to withdraw. And now, here they were, stuck with an insurrection. The armed students were few in number—I reckoned there were about 200.

A woman made a signal to follow her, which I did, at a few paces. We went down a side-street and, to my surprise, into the building of the United States Information Service. The janitor opened it up for us. The woman had been afraid to talk in the open. She said the place was full of spies. She was not from Kwangju herself—she had come down from Seoul at the start of the troubles, being a member, I supposed, of some dissident group. Now she was stuck here, terrified that they were all going to be killed.

She was desperate that the world outside should be told the truth of what was happening. Only if the foreign press reported the truth would there be any chance of saving the students. 'You are our corridor to life,' she said.

Later in the day, I kept being asked by people: 'Are you going to tell the truth about us?' Government propaganda had branded the insurrectionists as communists. They were not communists, they insisted. They wanted democracy. They wanted an end to the power of General Chun Doo-hwan and the KCIA.

Some people said they were not 'with' the students. They were not in favour of the use of arms. But they were of one voice in saying that the students were their sons, and that if the army came in the students would be put to death. That was why they kept saying: 'Tell the truth about us.'

I didn't meet up with any of the foreign journalists there, but afterwards everyone had had the same horrible impression of doomed children. A couple of school students took me round the hospitals in what turned out to be a vain search for casualties. There were reasons why both the wounded and the dead might be whisked away by their families, for many people wanted to hide that their own children had been involved. The disgrace would spread. Relatives would lose jobs. They would fall under suspicion. I remember my schoolboy companions saying that they too might soon be killed.

The day was frustrating. It was so hard to find anyone who spoke more than a few words of English. Hard, too, to find people who wanted to talk in public. When the driver finally said it was time to go, a part of me was relieved that I did not have the money simply to pay him off and stay. To the voice that said, 'Don't go now, coward,' another voice replied, 'You must only take calculated risks.' And: 'Anyway, you're a theatre critic.' And: 'These people have told you to go out and tell the truth about them.'

Etienne was not to be found. I knew anyway that nothing would make him leave now. We got in the car and drove along the wide, empty streets, the way we had come in. People were standing in doorways and on the low roofs of the houses. Suddenly I noticed we were driving straight towards a line of tanks and soldiers. Maybe we couldn't get out after all.

I tapped the driver on the arm. With astonishing calm, he took stock of the situation and performed a very slow U-turn. We tried a few side-streets and soon enough were out of the city and back in the hills. We remembered the bellboy's packed lunches. Neither of us had eaten all day.

The driver stopped in a small village, where he astonished me again by walking straight into the police station and asking if we might eat our lunches there. It was the last thing I would have expected to do in a police state.

As we ate, the driver chatted away to the policemen, who were friendly types and clearly eager for news of Kwangju. I suddenly thought: So that was it—the driver was an agent all along, and I was simply being used as his cover. Now he is making his report.

But later, as we drove along the expressway through the dark, I noticed that he and the other drivers always flashed their lights at each other to warn about check-points ahead. The people on the road seemed to be in prudent league against the forces of the state. Nor did it seem likely that the village police of Cholla province were playing much part in the military operation to clear up Kwangju. I liked the driver. He had done a great job. I was less happy about the job I had done.

The next morning, on waking, I phoned Reuters to introduce myself. 'Well, you've heard the news then, I suppose?' said a tired voice. 'It's all over. They went in last night and fought it out.'

A couple of hours after I had left Kwangju, the army had delivered its ultimatum. The students who were defending their building called to the people of the town to come out onto the streets. But the people stayed indoors. The journalists who had spent time with the students remembered one leader in particular as having been extraordinarily impressive. He had said he would die at his post. And the next morning they found him shot in the chest with the grenade he had been about to throw still in his hand.

Etienne's photographs told the last of the story—the beating into submission of the students, the mass arrests.

Photo: Patrick Chauvet (Sygma)

South Korean paratroops in Kwangju.

4

When President Park Chung-hee was assassinated on 26 October 1979, his place was taken by Choi Kyu-hah, who, while in no sense the power that Park had been, became the focus of expectations. He was going to rewrite the constitution. People saw the chance of having a democracy.

General Chun Doo-hwan, who headed the Armed Forces Security Command, was placed in charge of investigating Park's assassination. Instead, on 12 December 1979, Chun mounted a coup with the aid of General Roh Tae-woo, removing some twenty generals, and cutting short a series of hitherto promising military careers.

Quite what the future held was uncertain. There were three leading politicians: Kim Jong-pil, of Park's group; Kim Young-sam, from the opposition; and the hero of the students, Kim Dae-jung, the man who had once been kidnapped from exile in Japan and brought back to house arrest in Korea. Kim Dae-jung had stood against Park in 1971. His capture in 1973 might well have led to his death, being thrown overboard in the Sea of Japan, but an American plane spotted the KCIA boat, and diplomatic pressure saved him.

By the spring of 1980, the so-called Seoul Spring, the pressure for democratization was very strong. The business community, uncertain which of the leading candidates to support, dug into its pockets and supported them all. The kind of democracy being talked about was not, at least in the eyes of the business community, anything radical, idealistic or necessarily libertarian. The military was anachronistic. That was the trouble with it. People felt they had outgrown dictatorship, censorship and the other forms of repression. The military was diverting attention and effort away from the development of a modern society.

But as people talked, debated, demonstrated over these issues, General Chun was moving towards total power. In April, he was made acting head of the KCIA. On 17 May he arrested all the key democratic leaders and extended martial law. The next day he sent in the paratroopers to Kwangju and the killings began. The insurrection that followed, and its crushing, marked the end of the Seoul Spring.

People talked, unrealistically, about Chun being made to take the blame. But Chun was unstoppable. A week after crushing Kwangju he relinquished his post in the KCIA: he no longer needed it. He became head of the Standing Committee for National Security Measures—which exerted military control over the civilian government. By mid-August, Kim Dae-jung was on trial—*he* would be made to take the blame for Kwangju. By the end of the month, Chun was 'temporary president'. The next year he was 'elected' president.

The students detested and feared Chun. The businessmen looked on him with distaste and apprehension. I remember a man asking me, in those days, wasn't it true that we in England had once had a character called Cromwell, and hadn't he, well, not been such a bad thing after all? This was said in a spirit of weariness which seemed to mean: maybe we *have* to suffer Chun, maybe it's just a stage we have to go through, as other countries have suffered before us.

5

Chun's Fifth Republic was a triumph—economically. And a part of that triumph expressed itself in the architecture of the dictatorship: the grandiose zoo outside of Seoul, with its staggering car-park; the Great Hall of the Nation, with its adjacent museum of the Korean struggle against the Japanese and its hideous chamber of Japanese horrors; and then, above all, the remodelling of the capital for the Olympic Games, with so many facilities that the world could not wait to participate.

All this was consistent with Chun's vision of himself as the sporting man of destiny, the goalkeeper general, the referee. There was also a totemic significance to the Games. It is felt that it was the Tokyo Olympics that marked the moment when Japan took its place among the great nations of the post-war world, and it is a deeply held belief, in the obscurest regions of Korean thought, that

Chun Doo-hwan's mother had produced other sons, but they died. Because of this, Mr Chun was thinking of leaving her. Then Mrs Chun had a dream in which three men and one woman walked down a rainbow to her house. The first man was clad in cobalt blue. The second man had broad shoulders and a majestic face and a crown on his head. This man was her next son but one, and he was christened Doo-hwan. He was born with a dark spot on his right wrist, which was connected with another premonitory dream in which Mrs Chun had tried to catch the moon in her skirt. This birthmark earned Chun the nickname Spotty.

When Spotty was one year old, a monk came begging at his home. Mrs Chun gave the monk a handful of barley. He lingered at the gate, as if wanting to say something. Later a neighbour came running to Mrs Chun, exclaiming, 'I overheard the monk saying to himself that you would see one of your sons grow up to be a great man, but your buck teeth might hinder that.'

Mrs Chun chased the monk and asked what he had meant. The monk said, 'I wanted to tell you that your physiognomy indicates you are going to be the mother of a great man, but your protruding front teeth may get in the way. Being a novice monk yet, I had no nerve to say that before. Anyway, may Buddha bless you!'

Mrs Chun decided to get rid of her teeth. She tied herself to one of the log pillars of the house and struck it hard, thinking: 'I'll do anything for my children, no matter what!'

She lost the teeth, but was ill for two and a half months.

Retold from *Chun Doo-hwan, Man of Destiny* by Cheon Kum-sung, translated by W.Y. Joh.

a great future lies in store for the divided country. After the Olympics, Korea can take its rightful place in the world.

As the plans for the Olympics progressed, many people expected Chun to retire in the post-Games euphoria. He had made emphatically public his desire to be the first president of South Korea to enjoy a peaceful transition from power. Now here he was saying he would step down *before* the Games. And everyone was certain he would fix the succession.

Thus it was that an immensely complex set of rival plans began to shape the future of the nation: Chun and his one-time Sports Minister Roh Tae-woo, planning to install the stadiums, the roads, the underground, the succession of power; and the opposition, planning to install the democracy—*their* contribution to the modernization of the country. And another thing had happened: a popular uprising had overthrown President Marcos in 1986. A bloodless revolution! Filipinos, notably sensitive to the way they are treated around the world, began to report that in South Korea they were considered celebrities.

Kim Dae-jung, whom I interviewed under house arrest, was very alert to the Filipino comparison. Like Ninoy Aquino, he had been condemned to death, allowed into exile in the United States and had then decided, after Ninoy's assassination, to 'do a Ninoy' and return to his country. That had been in February 1985. Now he was full of talk about people power.

I remember sitting in the garden of the Toksugung Palace near the City Hall. There were rumours of disturbances outside, and police had been placed near the palace gates. One plainclothes man was keen to talk.

In a short while he knew where I came from, what hotel I was staying in and what my job was. That seemed par for the course. When I told him that I now lived in the Philippines, his interest became intense. He asked me what I thought of his country. I told him what had long been the truth—that I liked his country and his people very much. When he asked what I thought of the political situation, I made some kind of diplomatic reply. I had only, after all, been here twice before in my life—once for a quick visit as a tourist and once in 1980.

The date hung in the air between us.

'Yes,' I said, 'it was at the time of Kwangju.'

'You were *there*?'

I changed the subject and asked about him. He had been a sociology student. Now he was doing his national service. His job today was to keep an eye out in the direction of the American Ambassador's residence. I asked him what he would do after finishing his national service. He said he would resume his studies.

I asked him why were the students so angry now. He said in a measured way, 'Because *they* think they are the only hope for democracy.'

And from then on there seemed to be an understanding between us: if I refrained from asking him *his* views, he would tell me what some people thought. For instance, he said that *some* people were very shocked at Kim Dae-jung's announcement that he would not stand in a direct presidential election. *Some* people hoped that he would change his mind.

Of course there was always the possibility that I was being egged on to say something subversive. But what I felt, during our conversation, was that I was meeting a man in a very common predicament. He had to sit out his national service. In the end, he would return to university and be able to speak for his former beliefs. Today, however, his job was to stop the students demonstrating. He couldn't do anything about that fact.

In exchange for what he had told me, I told him what little I knew about Kwangju. And he made absolutely no comment.

One Day in June 1987

'They don't use guns or truncheons, particularly,' said somebody's ambassador, 'but they do use an awful lot of tear-gas. And it's terrible. It sticks to your clothes and your skin. And they fire it practically at point-blank range.' The ambassador sneezed. 'There,' he said, 'it's begun already.' And he looked vaguely out of the sealed window.

I couldn't smell anything. I could hear in the distance the broadcast voices of the opposition, calling out like muezzins over downtown Seoul, but this was hours before the demonstration was due to begin. My companion sniffed again. And then he began to elaborate, very elegantly, on a line of argument which was not uncommon among foreigners in Seoul: in the West, the two Kims (Kim Young-sam and Kim Dae-jung), being opposition leaders, were identified with the cause of democracy; but it would be quite wrong to believe that if either of them took power there would be democracy in South Korea. You had only to look at the way they dealt with their own followers to see that they were autocratic and uncompromising. A political party in South Korea is not a group of people with a common platform—it is a loose coalition around certain personalities aiming at power.

And yet if the argument between the ruling party and the opposition was simply about power, it seemed incomprehensible. Why would Kim Dae-jung have risked his life for so long, as he indubitably had? And why would the supporters of the Kims risk theirs? Why were so many people prepared to risk everything, exposing themselves not just to the possibility of torture and death, but also to the certainty that, if arrested, they would be banished to the margin of South Korean society?

I put this to the ambassador, but we did not get very far. A remarkable thing began to happen to him as we talked. He appeared to have been tear-gassed. At first he was too polite to show it, but soon he was coughing and his eyes were watering. I thanked him very much and left.

Back in my hotel room, I looked down at the adjacent building-site, a deep pit cut in the rock. Every afternoon they would set off little explosive charges, and I would watch the progress of the work. No doubt somewhere in this great exploded hole they would accommodate the 'room-restaurants' and high-class saunas for the daily comfort of the salarymen, along with the proliferating luxury shops. But the tendency of the city, as it modernized, was to simplify and drive the street-life, literally, underground, into an extraordinary network of granite-lined underpasses. You can walk through much of Seoul without emerging into the daylight more than once or twice.

Photo: James Nachtwey (Magnum)

Photo: James Nachtwey (Magnum)

Kim Dae-jung (top) and Kim Young-sam; (facing page) Roh Tae-woo.

Photo: Patrick Durand (Sygma)

At the nub of one of these underground arcade systems rises the Lotte Hotel, which was built by a chewing-gum magnate of a romantic disposition. (He named the chewing-gum and the hotel after the heroine of Goethe's *Werther.*) This enormous complex has doubled in size since I first saw it. I would never dream of staying at the Lotte, but on a cold day it makes an excellent place to take a walk—visiting the department store, the arcades, the bakery, the dentist's, the health farm, whatever you fancy.

Hotels like the Lotte are built to impress the Japanese (Seoul really doesn't bother to impress the Americans any more) and the show-piece is the atrium lobby-lounge with its large picture window behind which a waterfall cascades over a natural arrangement of rocks and trees. Late at night, when the band has finished playing and the bar closes down, they throw a switch—and turn off the waterfall.

On this day, a demonstration was due to start outside the Lotte Hotel at five in the evening and to make its way to the Anglican Cathedral, just the other side of the City Hall. But the cathedral had already been cordoned off the previous day, and the plaza in front of the City Hall was as usual forbidden to demonstrators. There were rows of riot police, with their black-leather lobster-tail helmets—the *Kagemusha* brigade, as we used to call them.

In the morning, the Kagemushas were joined by the snatch-squads, the plainclothes men in crash-helmets and matching parkas. Tens of thousands of men were going to stop the demonstrators from reaching the Anglican Cathedral—a simple enough task since the cathedral is in a little back-street.

Shortly before five, I put on my paper smog-mask and began to stroll towards the City Hall, looking for demonstrators. The police were all around, and the tear-gas was already strong. The journalists and photographers, who were by now used to the rules of rioting, had taken to wearing hard hats, gas-masks and plastic arm-bands identifying them as press. I was not properly kitted out.

When the tear-gas really hits you for the first time, and you burst into tears, the first thing you feel is sorry for yourself. You think: My God, I'm crying—a tragedy must have befallen me. Then, if you can bear to think at all, this weeping strikes you as funny—this sudden illusion of grief. And then, *then* you really do feel sorry for yourself.

Photo: Toshi Matsumoto (Sygma)

Photo: James Nachtwey (Magnum)

Outside the Lotte Hotel, I began to recognize members of the opposition. The demonstration was about to begin in earnest. But such was the strength of the gas, as the demonstrators came past me with their faces in their hands, I gave up. I couldn't see any more.

I went into the Hotel. I needed to talk to people. I had an article to write that night. Once there, I saw that it would be hard to leave, because the crowds were now rushing the revolving doors. I could see that even if I got into the revolving compartment, I might get stuck there, revolving, with a host of other people drenched in gas. A hideous fate.

I turned to the atrium lounge, with its high ceiling and its welcome, open space. A few foreign businessmen and tourists were sitting drinking there, served by beautiful ladies in tea-pot skirts. Sitting as far away from them as I could, I stank and wept by myself. The understanding ladies brought handkerchiefs, peanuts and beer. An absurd range of fancy drinks was available. The demonstration became smellably closer, the foreigners departed and the ladies burst into tears.

A riot broke out in the lobby. You could hear it, but it was literally true that if you walked from the atrium lounge into the lobby you couldn't see a thing. You were blinded. You could hear scuffling. You could hear people singing patriotic songs and the Korean version of 'We shall overcome'. It was hard to imagine how anyone could physically sing in such conditions.

The wall of tear-gas advanced. I found myself backed up against that gigantic plate-glass picture window, looking out at the waterfall, the miniature pines, the Japanese maples, the pretty rocks and the coi carp in the pool. I wished I could get out there, but we were all trapped.

There was a great noise of fighting in the lobby, and suddenly a nimble figure with cling-film over his eyes vaulted over a rococo glass-and-metal barrier and rushed across the lounge in my direction, looking over his shoulder as if in fear of pursuit. Reaching my chair, he crouched behind it, trembling and breathing heavily. I made him understand that the best thing for him to do (since no one had yet pursued him) was to sit down and join me for a drink. Taking the cling-film off his eyes, the student (he was in business management) suddenly became formal and immensely respectful. He accepted an orange juice and calmed down. When the time came to talk, I asked him the question which had been at the back of my mind all day: Did he and people like him believe that with the two Kims they would get democracy? What he said was just this: he didn't believe the victory of the two Kims would guarantee anything; it was simply that, under them, the country had a better *chance* for democracy. Nothing more.

7

It was a remarkable time, and I developed a routine. In the mornings, I relaxed in my room, reading Wordsworth. The students normally began rioting after lunch. By now I had my kit—gas-mask, hard hat, arm-band—which I would set off with, in the direction of the universities. Evenings were for writing stories and comparing notes with friends.

Seoul was everywhere contaminated. People moved into the upper storeys of hotels, only to find that the air-conditioning sucked up the tear-gas and made their rooms uninhabitable. One prayed for rain or the hoses of the municipal authorities. People stopped in the streets to listen to the loudspeakers of the opposition. Around the city there were illuminated signs counting down the number of days to the Olympic Games, which were now, with all the disturbances, in jeopardy. The Government and the ruling party made menacing noises. The situation had been deteriorating since 13 April, when President Chun had put a stop to the constitutional debate. On 10 June, Roh Tae-woo had been proclaimed the presidential candidate of the ruling party, which meant in effect that he was president-elect. From that day on, the country was in an uproar, which the widespread arrests did nothing to contain.

On 24 June, Kim Young-sam was finally able to meet with President Chun, to present the demands of the opposition. Their conversation was formal, meaningless and absurd: Kim Young-sam came away having made all the obvious suggestions, with cringing politeness, and without anything by way of results. But within the ruling party itself, the pressure for reform was beginning to be felt.

The riots had forced a new realism.

It was Roh Tae-woo who, in the end, made the public gesture of capitulation, and he did it with such style, and so absolutely, it took the breath away. Somebody somehow decided that the only way to outflank the opposition was to take all their central ideas and turn them into orthodoxy. From now on, Roh Tae-woo said, there should be direct presidential elections. There should be amnesty for political prisoners. Kim Dae-jung should have his rights restored. *Habeas Corpus* should be extended. There should be a free press. He—Roh Tae-woo—was making these demands, and if the president did not agree, then Roh would resign from his presidential candidacy and from his chairmanship of the ruling party.

So Roh went and stood before Chun, like God the Son before God the Father in *Paradise Lost*, ready to make the sacrifice of becoming a man, ready to be crucified at the ballot. And of course there was an element of the charade in this: Roh threatening Chun, Chun taking a couple of days to agree to Roh's demands. But there was also something real in the capitulation. From now on, the ruling party became the proponents of the demands of the Seoul Spring—albeit in their own subtle version—while the opposition was lost for a platform.

Throughout this period, a student called Lee Han-yol had lain in a coma, after having been hit on the head by a tear-gas grenade. Really it was astonishing that there had not been many more such casualties. But life is not cheap in Korea, and much attention had been focused on the fate of this young man.

On the day of his funeral, political rights were restored to Kim Dae-jung and 2,000 others. The placatory gestures of the government continued, and, to the surprise of many, the funeral procession was allowed to pass through the city centre unopposed. There was an enormous crowd. For once, you could see the strength of the opposition, rather than—as before—a confusing blur of running figures with streaming eyes. The traffic stopped. The City Plaza and the roads leading off it were filled. Every building was obliged by the students to lower its flags to half-mast. On the City

Photo: James Nachtwey (Magnum)

Hall, the Olympic Flag itself was removed. I doubt that most people—watching the scenes that day, awed by the solemnity and determination of the crowd—would have realized that the movement had reached its peak, that the insurrection was over.

Kim Dae-jung was now back in the legitimate arena. He would be able to revisit Kwangju and his own province of Cholla. He would hear the call of the people. He would have to run. And if he ran, it followed absolutely that Kim Young-sam would run. He, too, would hear the voice of the people. The rivalry of the two Kims was an ineluctable fact of political life. They dogged each other's steps. They copied each other's moves. They fought inseparably. For weeks and months they assured the people that they would sort this matter out—that there would be only one opposition candidate.

In the meantime, the retired four-star general, Roh Tae-woo, was hiring his image-builders and planning his campaign. He was to sell himself as the man with Big Ears, the good listener, the Ordinary Man. He would usher in—his advertizers said—a Great Era for the Ordinary Man.

On the Road with Mr Roh

Early one morning in December, I joined the press bus at the Democratic Justice Party Headquarters to accompany Mr Roh to Kunsan, Kim Dae-jung's birthplace, and Chonju: barnstorming Cholla province, enemy territory. It seemed an obvious thing to do. A rumour had gone around that someone was about to burn himself to death. That, if it happened, would be the picture of the day.

We drove down the motorway south towards Kwangju, and when we turned off we began to encounter strategically placed knots of loyal demonstrators at the roadside. The photographers began strapping on their helmets. We were warned that, the moment Roh finished his speech, we must all be on the press truck or we would be left behind. The warning seemed faintly bossy until you saw what was in store.

Along the approach road to Kunsan were lines of parked coaches. A crowd had been imported to protect Roh and his entourage from the real, hostile crowd they would meet. We dismounted from our coaches. Roh and his bodyguards took their places in the candidate's open truck, which was preceded to the rally site by a press truck. The streets were full and hostile. People crowded on roof-tops to see one of the men they held responsible for the Kwangju massacre.

It was extraordinary to be at a rally where ninety per cent of the audience was attending because it hated the speaker. Around the platform, the thugs from the snatch-squads chanted pro-Roh slogans. But as soon as Roh began speaking (telling the people of Cholla about a massive investment programme involving their part of the West Coast), the crowd turned its back on the speaker and began looking towards the periphery, where supporters of Kim Dae-jung were demonstrating.

At the end of the speech, we rushed to the press truck and the crowd edged closer. There were scuffles and tear-gas ahead of us. Mr Roh took his place on his open truck, surrounded by bodyguards with transparent shields. As we set off, he was wearing his usual smarmy smile. Then the rocks began to pour down. Mr Roh's shoulders hunched slightly. His face seemed to say: You don't hate me *that* much, do you? Oh, I see—you *do* hate me that much. Finally he disappeared beneath the plastic shields, and the two trucks wobbled at high speed along the road.

Several members of the press on our truck received minor injuries, and two were hospitalized. For the Korean press was very much despised—and the TV more so. Watching Mr Roh go through this performance, I thought: This is the first time in my life I have been literally stoned; I wouldn't have missed it for the world, but I don't want it to happen ever, ever again. The most astonishing sight, as we reached the coaches, was that of the plainclothes thugs rushing for their transport, dashing to get out of town. I was used to seeing these men evenly matched against the students—dangerous too. They were the most hated of the police and were popularly believed to have been recruited from the prisons. Here, however, not a man was going to wait a moment longer. We were all shooed out of town.

That afternoon, as we approached Chonju, we could see that most of the men were making their way towards the rally site. The Korean press corps was expecting more trouble here, in a city of some half million people, with many students. We waited for the Roh cavalcade to begin until suddenly it became apparent that it was not going to begin at all. Mr Roh was stuck in his hotel.

The rally site, by the railway station, had been ill-chosen. Small hills surrounded it, with a quarry and many other sources of rocks such as half-finished construction sites. There were the riot police, fantastically outnumbered by the crowd, trying to hold off the demonstrators, who were tearing down the Roh banners and burning them. There was tear-gas everywhere.

What ensued was like a medieval battle. When the crowd on the surrounding slopes saw that the police were on the retreat, they would come storming down, scree-running and thinking nothing of jumping an eight-foot drop off sheer rocks. Attack and counter-attack followed. Behind the police, the hired supporters performed their rehearsed routines, until it became clear that Roh could never show his face in this city. A group of students then sought him out in his hotel in the centre of town, where they kept up the hostile pressure through the evening. It was an impressive display of sheer, dogged detestation. Mr Roh said it was a pity for democracy. A member of the Government said publicly that Chonju should be punished for the insult it had delivered. But he had spoken out of turn in the Era of the Ordinary Man, and he lost his job in consequence.

When it came to playing the democrat, Mr Roh was more adept than his colleagues.

9

Election spending by the ruling party was so high it showed up in the money-supply figures. With money and gifts and then threats, the momentum for the ruling party was sustained. It was not a free election; it was a very expensive election. There was no expenditure ceiling for Mr Roh. I remember the drunk men, stunned with his generosity, at the end of his last big rally, and I remember walking back towards Seoul over the Map'O Bridge at sunset, watching the great drift of political literature into the Han River.

Each of the two Kims seemed confident. Either they would

win, or the public outcry at a rigged defeat would be so intense that, even if Roh 'won', he would lose. He would lose on the streets. He would be driven out by the righteous fury of the people. At his final rally Kim Dae-jung was particularly threatening on this point.

When the results began coming in, the outcome was obvious. Whether by fair means or foul, the ruling party had achieved a majority large enough to be decisive, but small enough to stand forever as a reproach to the opposition. From the early projections and through the night, suspiciously consistent but still—there it was—consistent, the figures said: If only the two Kims had got together, the opposition would have won. That there had been foul play, there was no doubt—but most people doubted there had been a sufficient amount of foul play to thwart the opposition. Whichever Kim you supported, the obvious fault lay with the other Kim, or with both.

It was Christmas. My interpreter was dejected. The ruling party began making menacing noises about anybody who failed to accept the results. When Kim Dae-jung appeared before the press he looked shocked and deflated. Before long both Kims would have to wear sackcloth and ashes, to apologize to the people they had betrayed. For the people themselves were not buying the story of election fraud: they were pointing to the crucial, brutal fact of the divided opposition.

After a few days the foreign press went home to their families, and the international observers left town. Those who had been expecting an explosion were disappointed. Apart from anything else, it was too cold for an explosion. And then there was all the shopping to be done.

Tired of Seoul, we went off to Mount Sorak and spent some days walking in the National Park. My interpreter was in love, and his girl-friend was thinking of becoming a nun. She had seen us off on the train, then gone to a convent for retreat.

I was reading Coleridge. My interpreter was writing poems in the next room. We walked in silence through the astonishing, pink granite ravines. Once we discussed the definition of happiness, which, said my interpreter, was to be free from the shackles of desire. We were surrounded by frozen, gurgling cataracts. The mountaineers hurried past us, properly equipped, but we were outclassed on the icy, difficult tracks.

'What happened in the Philippines?' asked my interpreter. I told him how Marcos had been declared winner, and how Cory had had herself proclaimed, in defiance of the results. Every day we watched the newspapers. My interpreter had heard that Kim Dae-jung would also have himself proclaimed.

We sat Christmas out, in the deserted resort, then went back to Seoul before the New Year influx.

Photo: James Nachtwey (Magnum)

Bruce Chatwin
Chiloé

The island of Chiloé is celebrated for its black storms and black soil, its thickets of fuchsia and bamboo, its Jesuit churches and the golden hands of its woodcarvers. Among its shellfish there is an enormous barnacle—the *pico do mar*—which sits on one's plate like a miniature Mount Fuji. The people are a mixture of Chonos Indian, Spanish and sailors of every colour, and their imagination churns with tormented mythologies.

The cathedral of Castro was built of corrugated sheet and painted an aggressive orange in honour of the Holy Year. Luggers with ochre sails were becalmed in the bay. At the café in the port sat an immensely distinguished, silver-haired man with long, straight legs.

He was a Sikh. Long ago, longer than he cared to remember, he was batman to an English colonel at Amritsar. One of his duties was to take the colonel's daughter out riding. Their eyes met. She was excommunicated by her family, he by his. Their life in England was a succession of hostile landladies. One day, he cut his hair and shaved his beard, and they went to South America. He and his wife had been happy on Chiloé. She had recently died.

'I would not have lived in any other way,' he said.

Two lakes, Lago Huillinco and Lago Cucao, all but bisect the island, flowing one into the other, brown water into blue, out into the Pacific. The lakes are the Styx of Chiloé. The souls of the dead are supposed to assemble at the village of Huillinco. The Boatman then ferries them to their destination.

The road to Huillinco was white and wound through fields of ripe grain. Winnowers shouted greetings as I passed. Silvery, shingled houses were encircled by pines and poplars. Hansel and Gretel would be happy to live here.

Under a tree of waxy white flowers a fat young man sat eating blackberries. Hector Dyer García was returning from the races. He had lost money.

'Do you know Notting Hill Gate?' he asked.

Around the turn of the century, Alfred Dyer-Aulock jumped ship and landed in the arms of a Chilote girl. On his deathbed, he told his family to write to their English cousins. They did not know how to do this. Hector dreamed of an unclaimed inheritance in a London bank.

'Or I shall have to go to Venezuela,' he said.

We walked slowly, stopping at a blue cottage to drink cider with a woodcutter's family. At dusk, we came to Huillinco—a cluster of houses, a jetty and the silver lake beyond. Evangelists with nasal voices were droning to a guitar.

Hector crept into his house as though visiting the scene of a crime. He had a wife. She was twice his size and twice his age. Shrieking abuse—between mouthfuls of cheese—she drew out his painful confession. He had lost on the horses the money intended for groceries.

I spent the evening with Hector and his friends, playing dominoes in the bar.

In the morning a milky fog smothered the settlement. Across the lake came the sound of rowlocks and the muffled bark of a dog. A man, rubbing the sleep from his eyes, said the ferry to Cucao would come at three in the afternoon.

I walked along the lake shore, amid mimosas, wintergreen and flame trees. Emerald humming-birds sucked at trumpets of scarlet honeysuckle. One shrub had bright purple berries. The country smelled of burning.

At three, the villagers sighted the ferry, a black speck at the far end of the lake. Horses with panniers were tethered alongside the jetty.

The people of Cucao disembarked their produce: bales of black wool, mussels and trusses of seaweed and shallots. The boatman was a tiny man with glistening brown skin and an almost circular mouth. He was one of the last pure-blood Chonos Indians.

Besides myself, the only passenger for Cucao was Doña Lucerina, a firm-jawed woman swathed from head to foot in black. She owned the only hostel in the village.

The boatman had started the guttering outboard when two boys ran to the shore carrying a white wood coffin. They were red-eyed from crying. They had gone to fetch a priest for their dying mother: he had refused to come. They sat a night and a day outside the priest's house: he refused to come. Then word came she was dead, still he wouldn't come. The weather was hot. The mother was rotting, unburied and unshriven.

'When did she die?' demanded Doña Lucerina.

'Friday.'

'At what hour?'

'Ten in the morning.'

'Heart?'

'Lungs.'

'Ah!' she gave a knowing smile. 'Tuberculosis! Bad diet. For tuberculosis you must drink milk. Then the disease cannot enter the bones.'

'She was ill for years,' said the younger boy.

'She should have drunk more milk when she was young.'

The boat glided into Lago Cucao. The boatman dropped the boys on a beach of white stones. We watched them, two black figures carrying the coffin to their homestead, through the dead trees.

At Cucao there were two wooden churches on a meadow: they might have been built by Early Celtic monks. Kingfishers flew back and forth. The boatman tied up beside a row of cottages. I paid him my obol. Doña Lucerina led the way along a sandy path: we brushed our legs against giant-leaved gunnera.

We climbed the headland. The setting sun coloured the Pacific rollers a milky golden green. The sands along the bay were black. A fishing boat, crossing the bar, was a black crescent in the foam. Doña Lucerina's house was long and low, with a roof of shingles and planked walls painted cream.

'All mine!' she gestured along the beach. 'Two hundred hectares, the house, and mines of gold. I have to sell it. My husband is sick.'

In the dark green kitchen sat her lodger, Don Antonio: a straight-backed old man with dark eyes glittering through a fuzz of eyebrow.

'Tell the young man some stories,' said Doña Lucerina. 'He wants to hear stories.'

In soft and musical Spanish, Don Antonio told of the Basilisk and the Fiura, the Sirens and the Pincoya.

'Ah! I love the Pincoya,' Doña Lucerina clapped her hands.

The Pincoya was a sea-nymph: a laughing girl who encouraged the shellfish to multiply. Sometimes you saw her dancing on the sands, her dress of seaweed shimmering with pearls and her flaming hair streaming in the wind.

'Tell him another, old man,' she said. 'Tell him about the King of the Land.'

'Long ago,' Don Antonio began, 'Cucao had everything—cows, horses, sheep, goats, everything—and the rest of Chiloé had nothing. One day a sheep was born with three horns, and its fame spread. A stranger came to see the sheep and stayed the night. In the morning the people woke to find all their animals gone. They followed the tracks and came to a river. There was an old man sitting on the bank.

'"Have you seen the thief who stole our animals?" they asked.

'"That was no thief," the man said. "That was the King of the Land."

'And ever since the people of Cucao have nothing and the rest of the island is rich.'

'And another one!' said Doña Lucerina. 'Tell him about Millalobo.'

'Do you remember the cottages by the landing-stage?' he asked.

'I do.'

'In the second cottage,' he went on, 'there lived a family—mother, father, daughter. We knew them well . . .

'One day the mother told the girl to fetch some water for coffee from the spring . . . *por un cafecito no mas*. The girl did not want to go: there was a stranger, she said, in the village. But the mother insisted and the girl did not come back. The mother called and called and searched everywhere. She came to the spring and there was blood . . . blood all around . . . *pura sangre*. The neighbours said yes, they had seen a stranger. He was as tall and fair as you are, Englishman. The mother knew that Millalobo had taken her daughter . . .

'A year later the girl came back with a baby in her arms. The woman was thrilled with her grandson, and rigged up a cradle. One morning, the daughter left the house, warning her mother not to look at the child. "Remember what I said, Mother," she repeated as she closed the door. But the woman was aching to see her grandson and rolled back the coverlet. From the waist down the baby was a seal. Then it changed into a star and bounced around the room, and out of the window, buzzing like a horse-fly.

'The girl heard the buzzing. She knew her husband had bewitched the child and sent it to live in the sky. She roamed the seashore crying, "Cucao! Cucao!" She walked into the water and slid under the surface . . .

'Millalobo built a palace for her at the bottom of the lagoon. Once a year he frees her and she floats to the surface, and when she sees the meadow and the churches, she breaks into song: "Cucao! Cucao! Cucaoooooooooooo!"'

'Now tell him about the Boatman,' Doña Lucerina insisted.

Don Antonio was tired now: but he stood at the window and pointed to a chain of three black rocks like stepping-stones at the far end of the bay.

'Those rocks,' he said, 'are the Boatman's Landing. I once knew a man who laughed at the story of the Boatman. He stood on one of the rocks and shouted, "Boatman! Boatman!" and the Boatman came.'

Night fell over Cucao. A full moon lit the surf. The fire of some gold-panners burned a hole in the darkness. I walked along the sands. I approached the Boatman's Landing but I resisted the temptation to call.

Nik Cohn
Immigrant

'Reagan's America does not hate foreigners. It just doesn't care for them,' I had heard. I wanted to see for myself, and so I spent time in the Immigration Court, thirteen floors up at Federal Plaza in New York, and watched the machinery of the Immigration and Naturalization Service (INS) at work. Scattered about an oblong space with no windows, the supplicants were jammed into rows of school desks, to keep them feeling suitably small, and there they waited to be called. And waited; and went on waiting.

Ali Akbar came from Iran. His father had been a colonel under the Shah, a professional pro-American, and when Ayatollah Khomeini came to power, he was imprisoned and tortured, his property was confiscated, and all his family were deemed public enemies. Ali Akbar himself was jailed three times for crimes never named, then press-ganged into the army and dispatched to the borderlands, there to wage Holy War on Iraq and expiate his sins through martyrdom: 'I was,' he told me, 'unglad.'

So he fled. With his wife and young son, he escaped to Turkey. They had neither papers nor travel permits, and the Turks refused them shelter. Ten thousand dollars, smuggled out to them from Iran, bought three forged Spanish passports and airline tickets to Montreal, but their flight developed engine trouble and was forced to land at JFK in New York. There, in December 1986, they asked for political asylum. The request was denied.

They were designated 'excludable aliens', a classification dreamed up by members of the Reagan administration to legitimize the rejection of the thousands of refugees from 'Baby Doc' Duvalier's Haiti who begged entry to Florida in 1981. The classification had since been extended to cover undocumented aliens world-wide, guaranteeing, as one observer noted, Equality of Injustice for All. The new policy was for automatic detention, to be followed by repatriation, without right to bond. The fact that such a procedure would often be tantamount to a death sentence was admitted, but not, the State Department believed, relevant.

To return Ali Akbar and his family to Iran was clearly an act of legalized murder. The INS, not willing to argue the point, resolved to send them back regardless, a ritual hand-washing which was abandoned only when Ali Akbar took refuge in a bathroom and hacked open both his wrists with a blunt disposable razor.

Thus Ali Akbar gained entry to the promised land. His wife and child watched him carried away on a stretcher, unsure whether he was dead or alive. They were then detained at the Viscount International, an airport hotel sometimes used as a holding pen by the Immigration and Naturalization Service, and later released with forty-five Canadian dollars. First they slept rough on the mid-winter Manhattan sidewalks and eventually found refuge with an Iranian community group. Only then, after countless enquiries had been stonewalled, did they learn that Ali Akbar had survived. Two weeks and 132 stitches after touchdown, he'd been removed from hospital to 201 Varick Street, an INS detention centre. And there he remained for over a year, awaiting final judgement.

The Varick Street lock-up was not designed for lengthy occupation. It provided no opening windows and no prison yard, no exercise facilities of any kind, no natural light, no fresh air. The food and the guards were notorious. So was the violence. Inmates slept fifty or more to a room. Most of them were convicted criminals awaiting deportation. The asylum-seekers were outnumbered four or five to one. There were between twenty and thirty of these, from Chad and Afghanistan, from Ghana and Nicaragua and Ethiopia, as well as from Iran. Nothing in their backgrounds had equipped them for such an ordeal. Many took sick.

Ali Akbar was one. When he was not beaten up by fellow-inmates who wished to steal his watch or take his turn at the phone, he was beaten up by the guards for, in law-enforcement jargon, *creating a disturbance.* More and more, his time was divided between visits to the infirmary and sojourns in MAX, i.e. solitary confinement.

It was understandable. In the authorities' view, he was a trouble-maker. All asylum-seekers, in fact, were trouble-makers, since they refused to accept that they were criminals, not political cases, and submit meekly to the penalties. On the contrary, the harsher their punishment, the more strident their protests. They organized petitions, chanted, threw food. There'd been a riot the previous January, with detainees smashing windows and shrieking slogans—'We are human beings! Help us!'.

In November 1987, seventeen long-term prisoners from seven different nations, all other avenues of dissent exhausted, declared a hunger strike. Their proclamation was hand-printed:

> WE THE UNDERSIGNED DETENEES [*Sic*] WHO HAVE APPLIED FOR REFUGEE, POLITICAL ASYLUM . . . HAVE BEEN DETAINED FOR SEVERAL MONTHS, AND CAN NO MORE BE DETAINED FOR THE REST OF OUR LIVES . . . PLEASE COME TO OUR AID . . . WITH KIND REGARD . . .

Ali Akbar was among the ringleaders. He was frail to begin with, his legs had been kicked and clubbed with night-sticks until he had trouble walking, his hands shook in spasms, and his eyes darted to and fro constantly. Still, on the afternoon I visited him, he made no play for pity. Perhaps he was too ill and too exhausted. Perhaps it wasn't his style. Either way, the facts were left to speak unaided. All incidents were relayed in the same monotone. But there was no mistaking his resolve. If he remained in Varick Street much longer, he believed, he would be dead or permanently harmed. He had nothing left to lose.

Official response to the hunger strike was apoplectic. Ali Akbar, when he tried to phone his wife against guards' orders, was first shackled to his bed, then hauled off to the infirmary where he sustained his fast for nineteen days, and was force-fed through tubes. A few days' respite, and he went on strike a second time. But by now his case was finally approaching settlement, not, both government and his own lawyer concurred, because of any pressure exerted by his protests, but simply because his number had come up. A curt three-page opinion found in his favour. His request for asylum was granted; he was released, three days after Christmas.

His fellow strikers enjoyed no such luck. But the manifesto had made its mark. The *Village Voice* had written of the case; human rights groups had become involved. In the long run, government shame at bad publicity if too much human damage was documented, or United Nations protocol too baldly mocked, would prevail where decency went for naught. The majority of the Varick Street refugees would win release, and in time become assimilated as new Americans. Then a fresh batch would replace them, and the waltz begin anew.

Photo: Sylvia Plachy

The last time I saw Ali Akbar, he was ill, utterly used up. When I asked if he could summarize all that had happened to him, he just shook his head and spread his shaking hands palms-up on the table that divided us: 'I am,' he said, 'unglad.'

'Let me explain one thing,' said immigration lawyer Irving Edelman. 'The INS, in the majority of cases, is not vicious. What it is, it's indifferent. Because of the way it's set up, and the signals it gets from on top, it simply doesn't care. Or to be exact, it can't care. The caseload is just too heavy and the personnel too lightweight, the whole system too dehumanized. Barely to keep ticking over, day by day, is already more than it can handle. If it had to show concern as well, the circuits would blow out completely.'

The majority of cases are not as wrenching as that of Ali Akbar. Back in the Federal Plaza waiting room, where I'd been introduced to his story, high tragedy was interspersed with black comedy, even farce: 'Humanity with its pants down,' Edelman called it. In the trade Edelman was known as one canny lawyer, a true J. Cheever Loophole, whose gifts in finagling and hair-splitting ran second to none; but also as something of a rogue elephant, a runaway train spreading havoc and confusion.

'Irving Edelman,' one colleague said, 'is a slime.'

'But a very fine slime,' said another.

His sin, I gathered, was that he did not play the game; failed to pay due devotion to profit, status and the majesty of the law. Instead, he brought to court a pure pagan joy in combat, much wit, more nerve, a motormouth that never tired, and no sense of shame whatever. At college he had studied Restoration Comedy and he approached immigration cases as though they were similar evidence of human absurdity.

Much of the levity derived from fraud. Most of the standard dodges—arranged marriages, farm workers with babysoft hands, families that overnight produced numerous grown-up children—were old and lame with over-use. But every so often there would be a new wrinkle.

One such, defended by Edelman, was the case of Luna Blanton. A large Guatemalan matron now living in Brooklyn with one husband, two children and some chickens, she spoke little

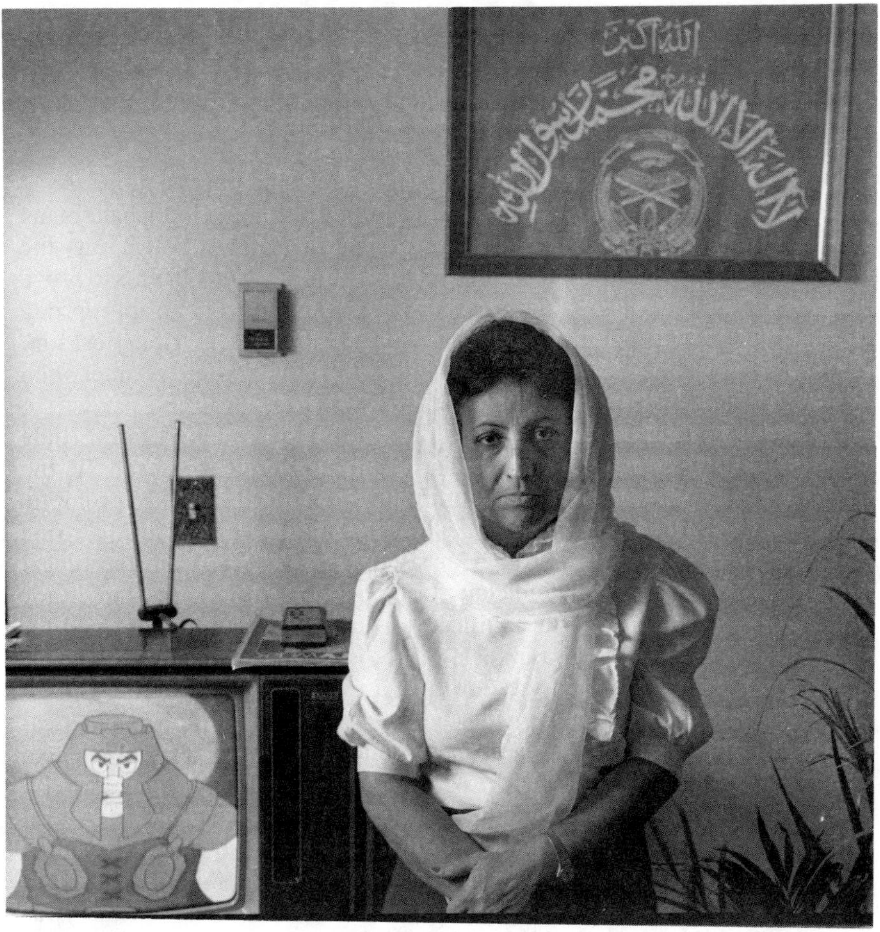

Photo: Sylvia Plachy

English and understood less, at least where the law was concerned. Her story stretched back many years.

It began with a black American sailor, name of Levon Blanton, who chanced to be drinking in some boondocks bar in Charleston, South Carolina, when he fell into conversation with a young Guatemalan, an illegal, rich in funds and imagination. As a merchant seaman, Blanton had passed through Guatemala many times, in particular the port of Puerto Barrios, which was the stranger's home town. What's more, he had the documents to prove it, and this it was that gave the stranger his idea. For an appropriate fee, he proposed, Blanton should recognize him as a long-lost son, a prodigal returned. Automatically, that would render him American street-legal.

So it was agreed, and there the real Levon Blanton, duly rewarded, exits. But for his freshly minted heir, Levon II, the odyssey had just begun. Returning to Puerto Barrios, he promptly set up trade, and sold off siblingships wholesale. For cash, anyone could become his brother or sister, and be American street-legal themselves. With judicious bribing of a government clerk, they even acquired birth certificates as official corroboration; and for years everything was sweet.

Greed proved the downfall. Levon II couldn't resist. Puerto Barrios became overrun by overnight Blantons, all America-bound. Even the American consulate, notorious for somnolence, woke up and took notice. An investigation was ordered.

It was too late. Before the investigators could make a move, all evidence had vanished without trace. The bribed clerk, arriving at work the next morning, was bundled into a car and driven off into oblivion, never to resurface: 'Let's just say his contract was terminated forthwith,' said Edelman. And that same night the clerk's office was ripped apart by a fire-bomb. Most of his files were destroyed outright, and the rest were exposed to the elements, since no roof remained. For weeks and months the Americans and Guatemalans dickered over who should foot the repair bills. Then the rainy season arrived, and the point became moot. It was as if Levon Blanton II, and all of his creations, had never been.

The Immigration and Naturalization Service did not bow gracefully; such is not its style. If Levon himself had escaped,

Photo: Sylvia Plachy

perhaps his alleged kin could be made to suffer instead. So Luna Blanton for one, though she had been a lawful resident for years and all of her existence was now American, found herself led into court and charged with immigration fraud.

It was, claimed Edelman, a travesty. This woman might or might not have connection with Levon Blanton II, and there might or might not have been some dirty work at the Guatemalan crossroads long ago, but since she had a Green Card, the burden of proof lay entirely with the INS. And where was said proof? 'Up in smoke. Down the toilet,' said Edelman, and there the defence rested.

The government could not produce one fact. So the action was dismissed, and the accused released. In the corridor outside the courtroom afterwards, however, she showed neither pleasure nor gratitude, but freed a luxuriant belch. 'I go now?' she grunted.

'*Vaya con Dios*, Luna Blanton!' said Irving Edelman, the Great Defender.

Case closed.

Anna Maria DePinto always wanted to be a nun. Though she grew up on Staten Island, she spent her summers as a child in Italy, at the family home at Rutigliano di Bari down in the south, and there she went each day to the nearby convent to wash and clean for the Sisters. Her female relations even teamed together to make her a replica habit. At thirteen, she could not wait to take her vows. Then, in Italy, she met Corrado Tritta, a fourth cousin.

He was the local Elvis: a strutter and a pistol, all flash, with scimitar sideburns, a whiplash sneer. He wore a white suit with a bright orange shirt, hip-huggers and loafers, and jewellery hung off him like Christmas decorations. Anna Maria called him the ugliest, just the grossest thing she'd ever seen. So they started to go steady. On her sixteenth birthday they got formally engaged and the next year, 1970, she brought him back to Staten Island, to be married: 'Real life,' as she says. 'No more dressing up, no make-believe—now we were strictly business.'

Corrado dispensed with the Presleyan vanities. He worked on a construction site, fathered a son and a daughter and dreamed of starting his own business. Five years passed unruffled. Then came the arrest.

He had committed a crime, it seemed. But he had not meant, Anna Maria swore, any harm. While at a neighbourhood karate club, he'd simply chanced to meet a man who possessed the secret of turning $25,000 into $175,000, no questions asked, no sweat. So Corrado and a friend put up $50,000, and when the promise fell through, it emerged that the friend's share was owed to a Mob loan-shark. To help keep his friend's kneecaps intact, Corrado lent his car for a series of armed robberies. His lawyer foresaw a two-year sentence, maybe less. It was, after all, a first offence. Corrado duly pleaded and was sent up for five to twenty years.

He served six. About half-way through, there was a deportation hearing, automatic for any non-citizen felon. Corrado had by then degenerated: 'a man mindless', he described himself, and he was too down to fight. His only question was whether he'd be permitted re-entry at some later date. To which the judge replied that he would be free to apply any time. On that understanding, Corrado offered no defence, and when he was eventually paroled, in 1981, both he and his family were returned to Italy.

For Anna Maria, the worst was still ahead. Rutigliano, so beloved on vacations, now seemed like being buried alive. Their new neighbours shunned them as Mafiosi. She was black-balled because she wore pants, drank a little wine and spoke her mind, and failed to act properly downtrodden, the way that southern Italian women should. Her own relatives, she knew, called her a Jezebel behind her back. After everything she'd been through, six years on her own, the loneliness and malice were more than her nerves could support. She fell apart. For months, she kept herself locked inside her room, confined to her bed: 'No woman, not even any person.' Corrado worked in another town and was gone five days a week. When he was home, she just cried.

The basic problem was that Rutigliano was not her home. America was. The same was true for the children, who were now growing up. After four years of exile, she was convinced that unless she went back soon, she would either kill herself or lose her mind forever.

Corrado applied for American re-entry, just as the judge had advised. And of course he was denied. By law, it could not be otherwise. So Anna Maria and the kids had to go without him and somehow, he vowed, he'd join them later.

It was March 1986. In Naples, $300 would purchase a visa to anywhere. Corrado opted for Canada and caught a flight to Toronto. He sneaked across the border, then reached Newark by plane. He was picked up by the INS as soon as he arrived there. Perhaps a phone call had been intercepted, perhaps someone had informed, but by entering illegally, Corrado had violated his parole, and back to jail he went.

The hearing was three months later. Corrado's only defence was to ask the judge what he himself would have done, if he could not live without his family and was not allowed to live *with* them. The judge made no reply but did release him, on $25,000 bond, against appeal.

The Trittas survived day to day. While Corrado worked construction in downtown Manhattan, their son Lenny, now fifteen, wrote pop songs and Nadia, ten, was a child model. With Anna Maria's health restored, they had a new home out on Staten Island, a mortgage and even some cash in hand. On the surface—good-looking and hard-working and God-fearing, unshakeable in love and faith—they could have passed for the American Dream family, at least until the next court date.

Seventeen years had passed since they'd arrived together in America. It had been twelve years since the arrest, nine years since the deportation order. Before the final decision, two or three years more would probably drag by. By then, within the span of this single, quite minor case, her daughter Nadia would have travelled from conception to confirmation. 'If only I'd've known,' Anna Maria said, 'maybe I'd have stayed a nun.'

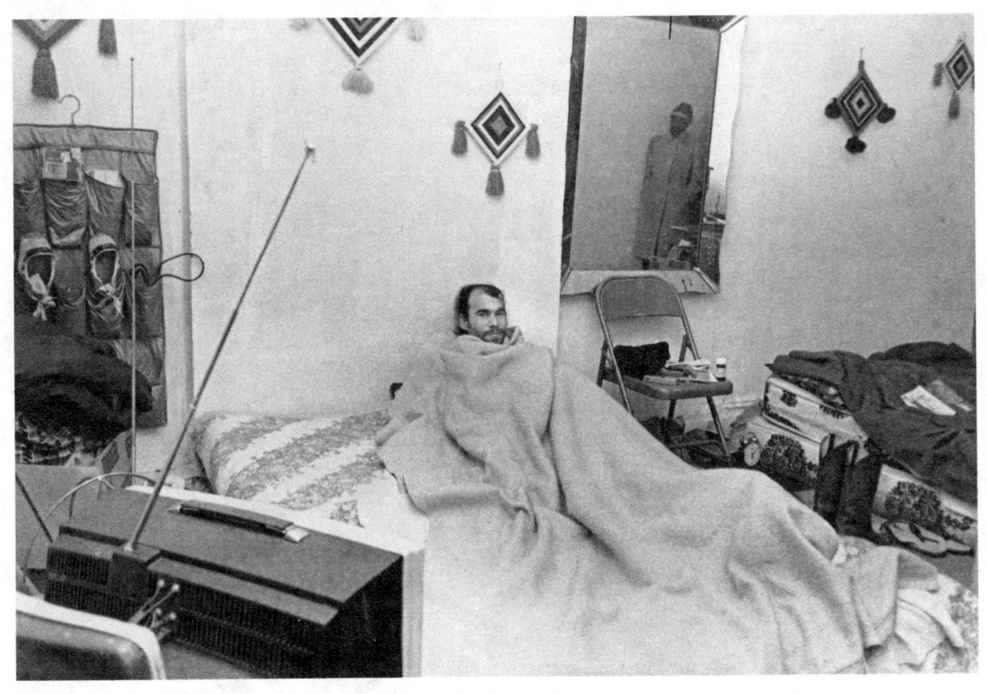

Photo: Sylvia Plachy

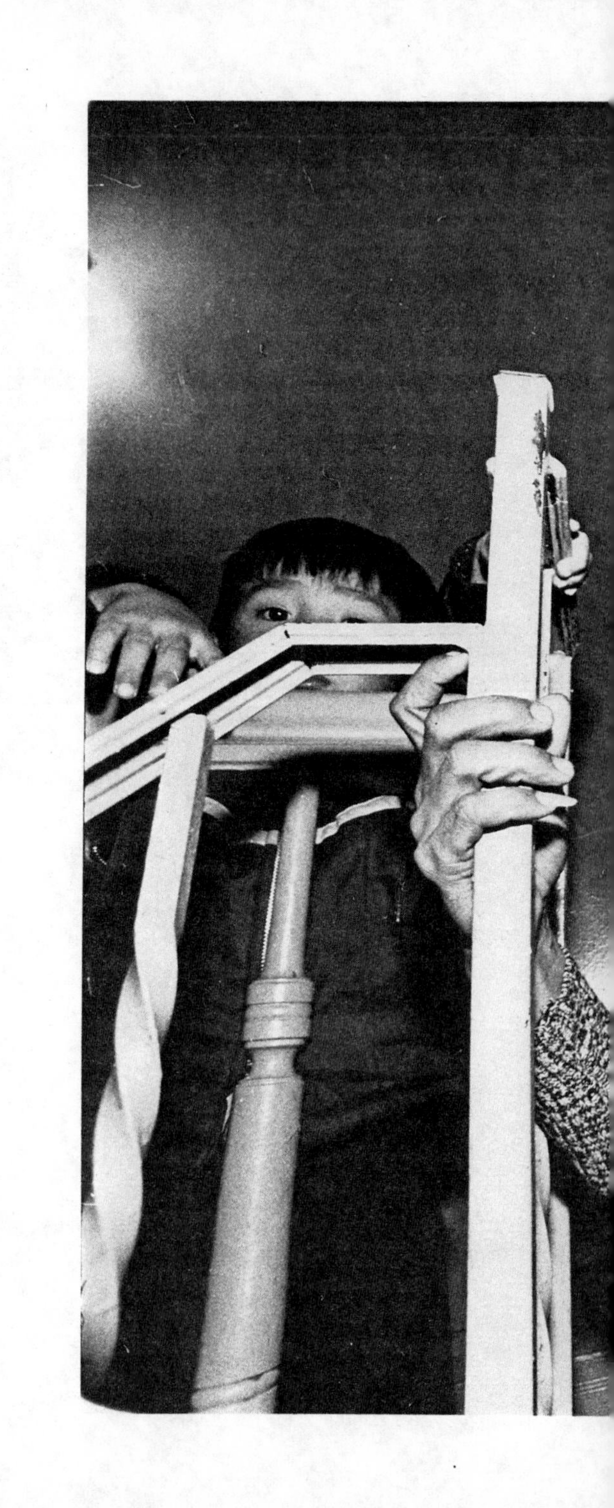

Photo: Sylvia Plachy

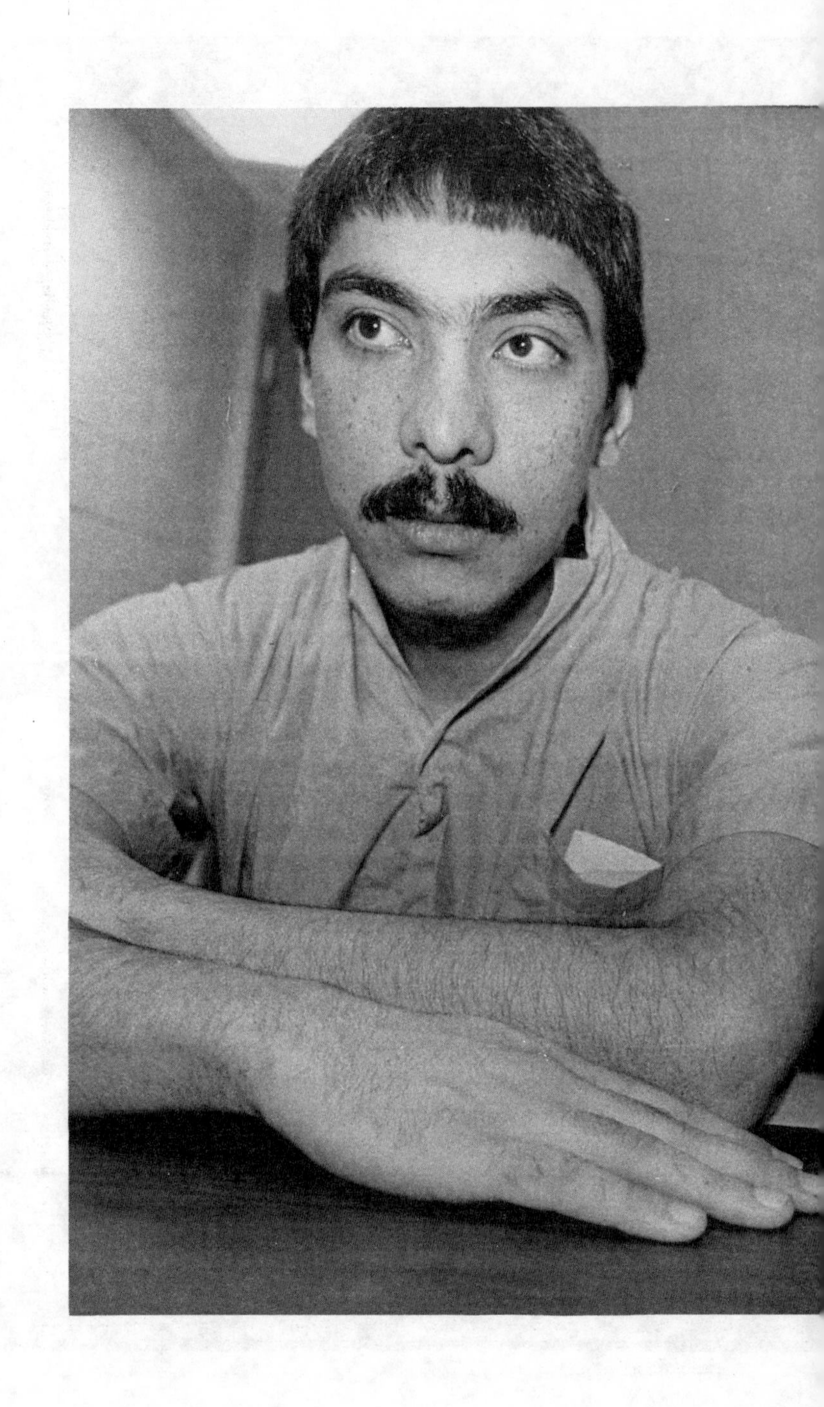

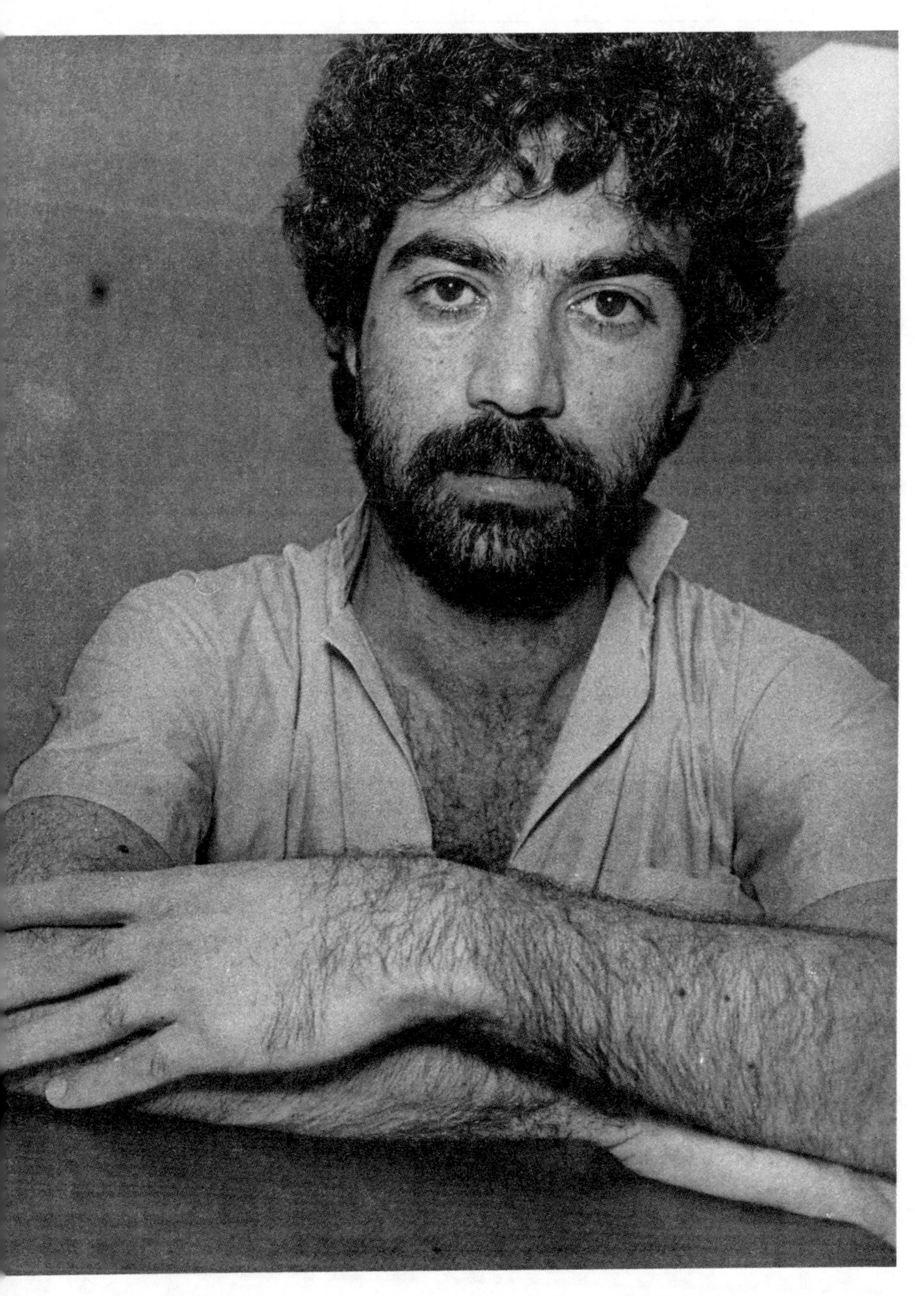

Photo: Sylvia Plachy

Another tale seemed archetypal. Mario Castro, a Salvadorean with thick pitch-black hair which he wore swept back and a hollowed and all-devouring Cholo stare, had been living and working as an illegal in Patterson, New Jersey, since March 1981. He had been an army sergeant and his body, even now when he was in his fifties, remained teak-hard. Out of long-time *macho* habit, it pleased him to challenge strangers to punch him in the gut, as hard as they liked, and try to make him blink. And of course they never could. But something way back in the eyes, a certain clouding, some reflex flicker like a camera shuttering, said that he'd been hit quite often and hard enough; that making him blink was no longer quite the point.

His problem was simply that he'd fought for the wrong man's army. He was a career soldier. But when El Salvador was swept by the military coup that installed a junta and would ultimately enshrine Duarte as shotgun president, his orders ceased to make sense. The notion of his army as a glorified police force, imposing civil obedience through terror, disagreed with him. So he quit.

Work then was scarce, money scarcer, and it took him three years to find a civilian job, in secret, in a petroleum factory. By that time, 1978, his only remaining ambitions were to raise his family of five sons intact, and for himself and his wife to survive to be old.

It was asking too much. In 1980 his eldest son, Herbert Mauricio, almost thirteen, began to run with a pack of older kids, anti-juntas who tested their manhood by pasting up dissident posters. For this the secret police first beat Herbert up, then confined him to house arrest, then abducted him for an improving session of torture. This involved such refinements as wadded papers shoved down the throat, all-over cigarette burns, and electrodes applied to the genitals. The aim normally was not to kill outright, merely to maim. But this time zeal must have overflowed, for the boy died. The naked corpse was dumped on the highway, near the family home, and when Mario Castro, who knew too much, went to claim it, the word was that he'd be next. He buried his son quickly. And fled.

His mother and his brother, who had departed for America years before, funded his escape. A hundred dollars took him to Mexico City in the back of a banana truck; $500 more bought his

Photo: Sylvia Plachy

passage in one of the massed convoys, one hundred people to a shipment, across the Rio Grande to El Paso. From there an eighteen-wheeler rode him into Los Angeles, a series of freight trains to New York, a gypsy cab safe to Patterson and seeming sanctuary. But it did not prove that simple. When Mario Castro applied for asylum, the INS said: 'Asylum from El Salvador? What for? Political problems?'

'You might say,' Castro replied, non-committal.

'But there are,' said the INS, '*no* political problems in El Salvador.'

His petition reverted to a state of permanent appeal. There it has lingered, for over seven years.

Castro has continued to live and work underground. During the day he labours in a packing plant; most nights he helps out at a downtown pizza parlour. Any surplus profits he sends home to his family in El Salvador. But he can't ever see them, of course, and due to mail censorship, he isn't even certain that they're coping. Now his sons are growing up fast, and his wife is growing old. He thinks of them constantly, he says, but cannot quite imagine them.

With the Amnesty, his days in limbo may be ending. If Castro is adjudged to qualify, as his lawyer deems probable, the family could be reunited sometime before 1989. Most likely, they would join him here in Patterson. Still he hungers to see his homeland once more, if only for a day: 'So long I have been gone,' he lamented, 'I don't even know who to visit in the graveyards.'

In the waiting-room, the immigrants took attrition for granted. Their only surprise was that anyone would be surprised. To be ignored if they asked directions to a bathroom, to be subjected to obscenities because they couldn't read a 'No Smoking' sign, in general to be treated as retarded or unclean—all of this, apparently, was a necessary down-payment on survival, on staying alive and in America. And for that, it was agreed, no price could be too high.

It was the one given. In every other respect—colour, country, creed—these people might have nothing in common. Some were convicted criminals, others sought political asylum, still others had overstayed their visas or were accused of Green Card frauds, and a few might even be mistakes, the victims of computer or human error. But this one bond was absolute.

I started asking what made the game worth the candle, precisely what was so great about America that it outweighed all losses, humiliations, terrors. My answers were stares or silence.

Only one man, an IRA activist, veteran of Long Kesh camp and now an alleged arms agent, could be bothered with even a one-line throwaway. 'More money. Less shit,' he said.

I remembered leaving Mario Castro. I said, 'Goodbye,' but he said, 'Adios.' He survived underground, never mingling with native Americans and his English was non-existent. As I went away, however, he called me back with three words, impeccably pronounced. 'God Bless America,' he said, and smiled, and softly shut his front door.

E. L. DOCTOROW
THE APPRENTICE

He had to have planned it because when we drove onto the dock the boat was there and the engine was running and you could see the water churning up phosphorescence in the river, which was the only light there was because there was no moon, nor no electric light either in the shack where the dockmaster should have been sitting, nor on the boat itself, and certainly not from the car, yet everyone knew where everything was, and when the big Packard came down the ramp Mickey the driver braked it so that the wheels hardly rattled the boards, and when he pulled up alongside the gangway the doors were already open and they hustled Bo and the girl upside hardly before they even made a shadow in all that darkness. And there was no resistance, I saw a movement of black bulk, that was all, and all I heard was maybe the sound someone makes who is frightened and has a hand not his own over his mouth, the doors slammed and the car was humming and gone and the boat was already opening up water between itself and the slip before a thin minute had passed. Nobody said not to so I jumped aboard and stood at the rail, frightened as you might expect, but a capable boy, he had said that himself, a capable boy capable of learning, and I see now capable of adoring worshipping that rudeness of power of which he was a greater student than anybody, oh and that menace of him where it might all be over for anyone in his sight from one instant to the next, that was what it all turned on, it was why I was there, it was why I was thrilled to be judged so by him as a capable boy, the danger he was really a maniac.

Besides, I had that self-assurance of the very young which was in this case the simple presumption I could get away when I would, anytime I wanted, I could outrun him, outrun his rage or the range of his understanding and the reach of his domain, because I could climb fences and hustle down alleys and jump fire-escapes and dance along the roof parapets of all the tenements of the world if it came to that. I was capable, I knew it before he did, although he gave me more than confirmation when he said it, he made me his. But anyway I wasn't thinking of any of this at the time, it was just something I had in me I could use if I had to, not even an idea but an instinct waiting in my brain in case I ever needed it, or else why would I have leaped lightly over the rail as the phosphorescent

---

Dutch Schultz.

water widened under me, to stand and watch from the deck as the land withdrew and a wind from the black night of water blew across my eyes and the island of lights rose up before me as if it were a giant ocean liner sailing past and leaving me stranded with the big murdering gangsters of my life and times?

My instructions were simple, when I was not doing something I was specifically told to do, to pay attention, to miss nothing; and though he wouldn't have put it in so many words, to become the person who would always be watching and always be listening no matter what state I was in, love or danger or humiliation or deathly misery—to lose nothing of any fraction of a moment even if it happened to be my last.

So I knew this had to have been planned, though smeared with his characteristic rage that made you think it was just something that he had thought of the moment before he did it as, for instance, the time he throttled and then for good measure stove in the skull of the Fire Safety inspector a moment after smiling at him in the warehouse in appreciation for his entrepreneurial flair. I had never seen anything like that, and I suppose there are ways more deft, but however you do it it is a difficult thing to do: his technique was to have none, he sort of jumped forward screaming with his arms raised and brought his whole weight of assault on the poor fuck, and carried him down in a kind of smothering tackle, landing on top of him with a crash that probably broke his back, who knows? and then with his knees pinning down the outstretched arms, simply grabbing the throat and pressing the balls of his thumbs down on the windpipe, and when the tongue came out and eyes rolled up walloping the head two three times on the floor like it was a coconut he wanted to crack open.

And they were all in dinner clothes too, I had to remember that, black tie and black coat with the Persian lamb collar, white silk scarf and his pearl-grey homburg blocked down the center of the crown just like the President's, in Mr Schultz's case. Bo's hat and coat were still in the hat-check in his case. There had been an anniversary dinner at Mori's down on Bleecker Street, five years of their association in the beer business, so it was all planned, even the menu, but the only thing was Bo had misunderstood the sentiment of the occasion and brought along his latest pretty girl, and I had felt, without even knowing what was going on when Mickey and Leo hustled the two of them into the big Packard, that she was not part of the plan. Now she was here on the tugboat and it was entirely dark from the outside, they had curtains over the portholes and I couldn't see what was going on but I could hear the sound of Mr Schultz's voice and although I couldn't make out the words I could tell he was not happy, and I presumed they would rather not have her witness what was going to happen to a man she might possibly have come to be fond of, and then I heard or felt the sounds of steps on a steel ladder, and I turned my back to the cabin and leaned over the railing just in time to see a lighted pucker of green angry water and then a curtain must have been drawn across a porthole because the water disappeared. A few moments later I heard one returning set of footsteps.

Under these circumstances I could not hold to the conviction that I had done the smart thing by coming aboard without his telling me to. I lived, as we all did, by his moods, I was forever trying to think of ways to elicit the good ones, the impulse to placate was something he brought out in people, and when I was engaged in doing something at his instruction I pressed hard to do my urgent best while at the same time preparing in my mind the things I would say in my defense in any unforeseen event of his displeasure. Not that I believed there was an appeals process. So I rode as a secret rider there at the cold railing through several minutes of my irresolution, and the strings of lights on the bridges behind me made me sentimental for my past. But by then we were coming down river into the heavier swells of the open water, and the boat began to pitch and roll and I found I had to widen my stance to keep my balance. The wind was picking up too, and spray was flying up from the prow and wetting my face, I was holding the rail and pressing my back against the side of the cabin and beginning to feel the light head that comes with the realization that water is a beast of another planet, and with each passing moment it was drawing in my imagination a portrait of its mysterious powerful and endlessly vast animacy right there under the boat I was riding, and all the other boats of the world as well which if they lashed themselves together wouldn't cover an inch of its undulant and heaving hide.

So I went in, opening the door a crack and slipping through

shoulder first, on the theory that if I was going to die I had rather die indoors.

Here is what I saw in the first instant of my blinking in the harsh light of a work-lamp hooked to the deck-house ceiling. The elegant Bo Weinberg standing beside his pointed patent leather shoes, with the black silk socks and attached garters lying twisted like dead eels beside them, and his white feet looking very much longer and very much wider than the shoes he had just stepped from. He was staring at his feet, perhaps because feet are intimate body parts rarely seen with black tie, and, following his gaze, I felt I had to commiserate with what I was sure he was thinking, that for all our civilization we go around on these things that are slit at the front end into five unequal lengths each partially covered with shell.

Kneeling in front of him was the brisk and impassive Irving methodically rolling Bo's pant-legs with their black satin side-stripe to the knees. Irving had seen me but chose not to notice me, which was characteristic. He was Mr Schultz's utility man and did what he was told to do and gave no appearance of thought for anything else. He was rolling up pant-legs. A hollow-chested man, with thinning hair, he had the pallor of an alcoholic, that dry paper skin they have, and I knew about drunks on the wagon what they paid for their sobriety, the concentration it demanded, the state of constant mourning it produced. I liked to watch Irving whatever he was doing, even when it was not as it was now something extraordinary. Each fold up of the pant-leg exactly matched the one before. He did everything meticulously and without wasted movement. He was a professional, but since he had no profession other than dealing with the contingencies of his chosen life, he carried himself as if life was a profession, just as, I suppose, in a more conventional employment, a butler would.

And partially obscured by Bo Weinberg and standing as far from him as I was but at the opposite side of the cabin, in his open coat and unevenly draped white scarf and his soft grey homburg tilted back on his head, and one hand in his jacket pocket and the other casually holding a gun at his side that was pointed with no particular emphasis at the deck, was Mr Schultz.

This scene was so amazing to me I gave it the deference one gives to the event perceived as historical. Everything was moving up and down in unison but the three men didn't seem to notice and even the wind was a distant and chastened sound in here, and the air was close with the smell of tar and diesel oil and there were piles of thick wound rope stacked like rubber tires, and pulleys and chain tackle, and racks filled with tools and kerosene lamps and cleats and numerous items whose names or purposes I did not know but whose importance to the nautical life I willingly conceded. And the tug's engine vibrations were comfortingly powerful in here and I could feel them running into my hand, which I had put against the door in order to close it.

I caught Mr Schultz's eye and he suddenly displayed a mouth of large evenly aligned white teeth, and his face of rude features creased itself into a smile of generous appreciation. 'It's the Invisible Man,' he said. I was as startled by his utterance as I would have been if someone in a church painting had started to talk. Then I found myself smiling back. Joy flooded my boyish breast, or perhaps gratitude to God for granting me at least this moment in which my fate wasn't in the balance. 'Look at that, Irving, the kid came along for the ride. You like boats, kid?' he said.

'I don't know yet,' I said truthfully and without understanding why this honest answer was so funny. For he was laughing now loudly and in his hornlike voice that I thought was terribly careless of the solemn nature of the occasion; the mien of the other two men seemed preferable to me. And I will say something more about Mr Schultz's voice because it was so much an aspect of his power of domination. It was not that it was always loud, but that it had a substantial body to it, it came out of his throat with harmonic buzz, and it was very instrumental actually, so that you understood the throat as a sound-box, and that maybe the chest cavity and the nose bones too, were all involved in producing it, and it was a baritone voice that automatically made you pay attention in the way of wanting a horn voice like that yourself, except when he raised it in anger or laughed as he was doing now, and then it grated on your ears and made you dislike it, as I did now—or maybe it was what I'd said that I disliked because I was joining in some cleverness at a dying man's expense.

There was a narrow green slat-bench or shelf hung from the cabin wall and I sat down on it. What could Bo Weinberg possibly have done? I had had little acquaintance with him, he was something of a knight errant, rarely in the office on 149th Street, never in the cars, certainly not on the trucks, but always intimated to be central to the operation, like Mr Dixie Davis the lawyer, or Abadaba Berman the accounting genius—at that level of executive importance. He was reputed to do Mr Schultz's diplomatic work, negotiating with other gangs and performing necessary business murders. He was one of the giants, and perhaps, in fearsomeness, second only to Mr Schultz himself. Now not just his feet but his legs to the knees were exposed. Irving rose from his kneeling position and offered his arm, and Bo Weinberg took it, like some princess at a ball, and delicately, gingerly placed one foot at a time in the laundry tub in front of him that was filled with wet cement. I had of course seen from the moment I had come through the door how the cement in the tub made a slow-witted diagram of the sea outside, shifting to and fro in viscous motion as the boat rose and fell on the waves.

I could handle the sudden events, getting baptized as by a thunderstorm, but this was more than I was ready for to tell the truth, I found I was not a self-confident witness here in contemplation of the journey about to be taken by the man sitting before me with his feet being cast in stone. I was working to understand this mysterious evening and the unhappy tolling of a life in its prime that was like the buoys I heard clanking their lonely warnings as we passed out to sea. I felt my witness was my own personal ordeal as Bo Weinberg was invited to sit now in a wooden kitchen chair that had been shoved into place behind him and then to present his hands for their tying. They were criss-crossed to each other at the wrist with fresh and slightly stiff clothes-line still showing the loops it came in from the hardware store, and with Irving's perfect knots between the wrists like a section of vertebrae. The joined hands were placed between Bo's thighs and tied to them cat's-cradle, over and under, over and under and then everything together was roped in three or four giant turns to the chair so that he could not lift his knees, and then the chair was twice looped to the laundry tub through the handles and the final knot was pulled tight around a chair-leg just as the rope ran out. Quite possibly Bo had at sometime in the past seen this scout-craft displayed on someone else for he looked upon it with a sort of distracted admiration, as if now, too, someone not himself was sitting hunched over in a chair there with his feet entubbed in hardening cement in the deck-house of a boat running without lights past Coenties Slip across New York Harbor and into the Atlantic.

The cabin was shaped like an oval. A railed hatch where the girl had been put below was in the center of the deck at the rear. Toward the front was a bolted metal ladder leading straight up through a hatch to the wheel-house where I assumed the captain or whatever he was called was duly attending to his business. I had never been on anything bigger than a row-boat so all of this, at least, was good news, that something like a boat could be so much of a construction, all according to the rules of the sea, and that there was a means of making your tenuous way across this world that clearly reflected a long history of thought. Because the swells got higher and longer, and everyone had to anchor himself, Mr Schultz taking the side bench directly opposite where I sat and Irving gripping the ladder leading upstairs to the wheel-house as if it were a pole on a subway train. And there was a silence for some time inside the sounds of the running engine and the waves, like the solemnity of people listening to organ music. And now Bo Weinberg was coming to life and beginning to look around him, to see what he could see, and who was here and what could be done; I received the merest glance of his dark eyes, one short segment of arc in their scan, for which I was incredibly relieved, not bearing any responsibility, nor wanting any, for these wheezing shifting seas or for the unbreathable nature of water, or its coldness, or its dark and bottomless craw.

Now there was such intimacy among all of us in this black cabin shining in the almost green shards of one work-light that when anyone moved everyone else noticed, and at this time my eyes were riveted by Mr Schultz's small action of dropping his gun in his ample coat pocket and removing then from his inside jacket pocket the silver case which held his cigars and extracting a cigar and replacing the case and then biting off the tip of his cigar and spitting it out. Irving came over to him with a cigarette-lighter which he got going with one press of his thumb just a moment before he held it to the tip. And Mr Schultz leaned slightly forward rotating the cigar to light it evenly, and over the sound of the sea and the grinding engine I heard the sip sip of his pull on the cigar and watched the flame flare up on his cheeks and brow, so that the imposition of him was all the more enlarged in the special light of one of his appetites. Then the light went out and Irving retreated and Mr Schultz sat back on the bench, the cigar glowing in the corner of his mouth and filling the cabin with the smell of smoke which was not really a great thing to be smelling in a boat cabin on the high seas.

'You can crack a window, kid,' he said. I did this with alacrity, turning and kneeling on the bench and sticking my hand through the curtains and unlatching the porthole and pushing it open. I could feel the night on my hand and drew it in wet.

'Isn't it a black night, though?' Mr Schultz said. He rose, moved around to Bo, who was sitting facing astern, and hunkered down in front of him like a doctor in front of a patient. 'Look at that, the man is shivering. Hey, Irving,' he said. 'How long till it hardens up? Bo is cold.'

'Not long,' Irving said. 'A little while.'

'Only a little while longer,' Mr Schultz said, as if Bo needed a translation. He smiled apologetically and stood and put a companionable hand on Bo's shoulder.

At this Bo Weinberg spoke and what he said was genuinely surprising to me. It was not what any apprentice or ordinary person in his situation could have said and more than any remark of Mr Schultz's to this moment gave me to understand the realm of high audacity these men moved in, like another dimension. Perhaps he was only admitting to his despair or perhaps this was his dangerous way of getting Mr Schultz's sincere attention; I would not have thought of the possibility that a man in his circumstances would feel he had a measure of control over how and when his death would occur. 'You're a cock-sucker, Dutch,' is what he said.

I held my breath but Mr Schultz only shook his head and sighed. 'First you beg me and now you go calling me names.'

'I didn't beg you, I told you to let the girl go. I spoke to you as if you were still human. But all you are is a cock-sucker. And when you can't find a cock to suck, you pick up scumbags off the floor and suck them. That's what I think of you, Dutch.'

As long as he was not looking at me I could look at Bo Weinberg. He certainly had spirit. He was a handsome man, with smooth shiny black hair combed back without a part from a widow's peak, and a swarthy Indian sort of face with high cheek-bones, and a full well-shaped mouth and a strong chin all set on the kind of long neck that a tie and collar dresses very nicely. Even hunched over in the shame of his helplessness, with his black tie askew on his wing collar and his satiny black tuxedo jacket bunched up above his shoulders, so that his posture was subservient and his gaze necessarily furtive, he suggested to me the glamour and class of a big-time racketeer.

I wished now in some momentary confusion of loyalties, or perhaps thinking only as a secret judge that the case had not yet been made to my satisfaction, that Mr Schultz could have some of this quality of elegance of the man in the tub. The truth was that even in the finest clothes Mr Schultz seemed badly dressed, he suffered a sartorial inadequacy, as some people had weak eyes or rickets, and he must have known this because whatever else he was up to he would also be hiking up his trousers with his forearms, or lifting his chin while he pulled at his collar, or brushing cigar ashes from his vest, or taking off his hat and blocking the crown with the side of his hand. Without even thinking about it he tried constantly to correct his relationship to his clothes, as if he had some sort of palsy of dissatisfaction, to the point where you thought everything would settle on him neatly enough if he would stop picking at it.

The trouble may have been in part his build, which was short-necked and stolid. I think now that the key to grace or elegance in any body, male or female, is the length of the neck, that when the neck is long several conclusions follow, such as a proper proportion of weight to height, a natural pride of posture, a gift for eye-contact, a certain nimbleness of the spine and length of stride, all in all a kind of physical gladness in movement leading to athletic competence or a love for dancing. Whereas the short neck predicts a host of metaphysical afflictions, any one of which brings about the ineptitude for life that creates art, invention, great fortunes, and the murderous rages of the disordered spirit. I am not suggesting this as an absolute law or even an hypothesis that can be proved or disproved; it is not a notion from the scientific world but more like an inkling of a folk-truth of the kind that seemed reasonable enough before radio. Maybe it was something that Mr Schultz himself perceived in the unconscious genius of his judgements because up to now I knew of two murders he had personally committed, both in the region of the neck, the throttling of that Fire Department inspector, and the more viciously expedient destruction of a West Side numbers boss who was unfortunate enough to be tilted back in a chair and having himself shaved in the barbershop of the Maxwell Hotel on West 47th Street when Mr Schultz found him.

So I suppose the answer to his regrettable lack of elegance was that he had other ways of impressing you. And after all there was a certain fluent linkage of mind and body, both were rather powerfully blunt and tended not to recognize obstacles that required going around rather than through or over. In fact it was just this quality of Mr Schultz's that Bo Weinberg now expounded upon. 'Think of it,' he said addressing the cabin, 'he makes this cheap dago move on Bo Weinberg, can you believe it? Only the guy who took out Vince Coll for him and held Jack Diamond by the ears so he could put the gun in his mouth. Only the guy who did Maranzano and bought him a million dollars of respect from the Unione. Who made the big hits for him and covered his ass for him, and found the Harlem policy he was too dumb to find for himself, who handed him his fortune, made him a goddamn millionaire, made him look like something else than the fucking lowdown *gonif* he is—this shmuck from the gutter. This bullet head. Listen, what did I expect, pulls me out of a restaurant in front of my fiancée? Women and children, anything, he doesn't care, he doesn't know any better, did you see those waiters cringing, Irving, you weren't there you should have seen those waiters trying not to watch him shovel it in sitting there in his Delancey Street suit that he bought from the signboard.'

I thought whatever was going to happen now I didn't want to witness; I had scrunched up my eyes and instinctively pressed back into the cold cabin wall. But Mr Schultz hardly seemed to react, his face was impassive. 'Don't talk to Irving,' he said by way of reply. 'Talk to me.'

'Men talk. When there are differences men talk, if there is a misunderstanding they hear each other out. That's what men do. I don't know what you came out of. I don't know what stinking womb of pus and shit and ape-scum you came out of. 'Cause you're an ape, Dutch. Hunker down and scratch your ass, Dutch. Swing from a tree. Hoo hoo, Dutch. Hoo hoo.'

Mr Schultz said very quietly: 'Bo, you should understand I am past the madness part. I am past the anger. Don't waste your breath.' And like a man who has lost interest he returned to his seat along the boat-wall across from me.

And from the slump of Bo Weinberg's shoulders, and droop of his head, I thought it might be true of a man of rank that he would be naturally defiant, and it might furthermore be true that he would exhibit the brazen courage of a killer of the realm for whom death was such a common daily circumstance of business, like paying bills or making bank deposits, that his own was not that much different from anyone else's, as if they were all a kind of advanced race, these gangsters, trained by their chosen life into some supernatural warrior spirit; but what I had heard had been a song of despair; Bo would know better than anyone there were no appeals; his only hope would be for a death as quick and painless as possible; and my throat went dry from the certainty that came over me that this was exactly what he had been trying to do, effect it, invoke Mr Schultz's hair-trigger temper to dictate the means and time of his own death.

So I understood of the uncharacteristic controlled response that it was so potent as to be merciless; Mr Schultz, he had made his very nature disappear, becoming the silent author of the tugboat, a faceless professional, because he let Bo's words erase him and had become still and thoughtful and objective in the approved classical manner of his henchman Bo Weinberg, as Bo, swearing and ranting and raving, had seemed to become him.

In my mind it was the first inkling of how a ritual death tampers with the universe, that inversions occur, everything flashes into your eyes backwards or inside out, there is some kind of implosive glimpse of the other side, and you smell it too, like crossed wires.

'Men talk, if they are men,' Bo Weinberg said now in an entirely different tone of voice. I could barely hear him. 'They honor the past, if they are men. They pay their debts. You never paid your debts, your deepest debts, your deepest debts of honor.

The more I done for you, the more like a brother I been, the less I have counted to you. I should have known you would do this, and for no more reason than you are a welcher who never paid me what I was worth, who never paid anybody what they are worth. I protected you; I saved your life a dozen times, I did your work and did it like a professional. I should have known this was the way you would make good on your debt, this is the way Dutch Schultz keeps the books, trumping up the wildest cockamamie lie just to chisel, a cheap chiseller chiselling every way he can.'

'You always had the words, Bo,' Mr Schultz said. He puffed on his cigar and took his hat off and reblocked it with the side of his hand. 'You got more words than me, being having been to high school. On the other hand I got a good head for numbers, so I guess it all evens out.'

And then he told Irving to bring up the girl.

And up she came, her marcelled blonde head, and then her white neck and shoulders, as if she was rising from the ocean. I had not before in the darkness of the car gotten a really good look at her, she was very slender in her cream-white evening gown hanging by two thin straps, and in this dark and oily boat, totally alarming, white with captivity, staring about her in some frightened confusion so that prophecies of an awful evil despoilage filled my chest, not just of sex but of class, and a groan like a confirmation of my feeling strangled in the throat of Bo Weinberg, who had been cursing a stream of vile oaths at Mr Schultz and who now strained at his ropes and shook his chair from side to side until Mr Schultz reached in his coat pocket and brought the grip of his pistol smartly down on Bo's shoulder and the girl's pale blue eyes went wide as Bo howled and lifted his head in pain and then said from his squeezed face of pain that she shouldn't look, that she should turn away and not look at him.

Irving coming up the stairs behind her caught her as she began to fold and set her down in the corner on a cushion of piled tarpaulin and leaned her back against cylinders of coiled line, and she sat on her side with her knees drawn and her head averted, a beautiful girl, I was able to see now, with a fine profile, as in the aristocracy of my imagination, with a thin nose and under it a lovely dimpled crescent curving out downward to a mouth which from the side was full-lipped in the middle and carved back to no more than a thin line at the corner, and a firm jaw-line and a neck that curved like a waterbird's, and—I dared to let my eyes go down—a thin fragile chest, with her breasts unencumbered as far as I could determine by any undergarment, being slight, although apparent at the same time under the shining white satin of her *décolletage*. Irving had brought her fur wrap along and draped it now over her shoulders. And all of a sudden it was very close in here with all of us, and I noticed a stain on the lower part of her gown, with some matter stuck to it.

'Threw up all over the place,' Irving said.

'Oh Miss Lola, I am so sorry,' Mr Schultz said. 'There is never enough air on a boat. Irving, perhaps a drink.' From his coat pocket he withdrew a flask encased in leather. 'Pour Miss Lola out a bit of this.'

Irving stood with his legs planted against the rock of the boat and unscrewed from the flask a metal cap and precisely poured into it a shot of neat and held it out to the woman. 'Go ahead, Missy,' Mr Schultz said. 'It's good malt whiskey. It will settle your stomach.'

I couldn't understand why they didn't see she had fainted but they knew more than I did, the head stirred, the eyes opened and all at once in their struggle to come to focus betrayed my boy's romance: she reached out for the drink and held it and studied it and raised it and tossed it back.

'Bravo, sweetheart,' Mr Schultz said. 'You know what you're doing, don't you? I bet you know how to do just about everything, don't you? What? Did you say something, Bo?'

'For Godssake, Dutch,' Bo whispered. 'It's over, it's done.'

'No, no, don't worry, Bo. No harm will come to the lady. I give you my word. Now Miss Lola,' he said, 'you can see the trouble Bo is in. You been together how long?'

She would not look at him or say a word. The hand in her lap went slack. The metal screw cap rolled off her knee and lodged in a crack of the decking. Immediately Irving picked it up.

'I had not the pleasure of meeting you before this evening, he never brought you around, though it was clear Bo had fallen in love, my bachelor Bo, the scourge of the ladies, it was clear he had gone head over heels. And I see why, I do most certainly see why. But he calls you Lola and I am sure that is not your name. I know all the girls named Lola.'

Irving passed forward, handing the flask to Mr Schultz, and continuing, and it was at this moment an uphill walk, the boat riding a run of wave prow-up, and he reached the forward ladder and turned to wait with all of us, watching the girl, who would not answer as the boat dropped under us, but sat now with two streams of tears silently coursing down her cheeks, and all the world was water, inside and out, while she didn't speak.

'But be that as it may,' Mr Schultz went on, 'whoever you are you can see the trouble your Bo is in. Right, Bo? Show her how you can't do certain things anymore in your life, Bo. Show her how the simplest thing, crossing your legs, scratching your nose, it can't be done anymore by you. Oh yeah, he can scream, he can shout. But he can't lift his foot, he can't open his fly or unbuckle his belt, he can't do much of anything, Miss Lola. Little by little he is taking leave of his life. So answer me now, sweetheart. I'm just curious. Where did you two meet? How long you been lovebirds?'

'Don't answer him!' Bo shouted. 'It's nothing to do with her! Hey Dutch, you're looking for reasons? I can give you all the reasons in the world and they all add up to you're an asshole.'

'Aah that is such bad talk,' Mr Schultz said. 'In front of this woman. And this boy. There are women and children here, Bo.'

'You know what they call him? Shortpail. Shortpail Schultz.' Bo cackled with laughter. 'Everyone has a name and that's his. Shortpail. Deals in this brewed cat-piss he calls beer and doesn't even pay for it. Chintzes on pay-offs, has more money than he knows what to do with and still nickels and dimes his associates. An operation this size, beer, unions, policy, runs it like some fucking candy store. Am I right, Shortpail?'

Mr Schultz nodded thoughtfully: 'But look, Bo,' he said. 'I'm standing here and you're sitting there and you're all finished, and who would you rather be at this moment, Mr Class Act Bo Weinberg? Moves on the man he works for? That's class?'

'May you fuck your mother flying through the air,' Bo said. 'May your father lick the shit of horses off the street. May your baby be served to you boiled on a platter with an apple in its mouth.'

'Oh, Bo,' Mr Schultz rolled his eyes upward. He lifted his arms out and his palms up and made mute appeal to the heavens. Then he looked back at Bo and let his arms fall to his sides with a slap. 'I give up,' he muttered. 'All bets off. Irving, is there another cabin down there that has not been occupied?'

'Cabin aft,' Irving said. 'The back end,' he said in explanation.

'Thank you. Now, Miss Lola, would you be so kind?' Mr Schultz reached out to the seated woman as if they were at a dance. She gasped and folded herself back away from his hand, bringing her knees up in the gown and pressing back, which made Mr Schultz look for a moment at his hand as if he was trying to see what about it was so repugnant to her. We all looked at his hand, Bo from under his lowering brow while at the same time making strange strangling noises, his ears and neck turning red with the effort to burst Irving's ropes. Mr Schultz had stubby fingers, a plump meaty rise where the thumb and forefinger joined. His nails needed a manicure. Sparse colonies of black hair grew behind each knuckle. He yanked the woman to her feet so that she cried out and held her by the wrist while he turned to face Bo.

'You see, Missy,' he said though he was not looking at her, 'since he won't make it easier we'll have to do it for him. So he couldn't care less when the time comes. So he'll be only too happy.'

Pushing the girl in front of him, Mr Schultz descended to the deck below. I heard her slip on the stairs and cry out, and then Mr Schultz telling her to shut up, and then a thin, extended wail, and then a door slamming, and then only the wind and the plash of water.

I didn't know what to do. I was still sitting on the side-bench, I was bent over and gripping the bench with my hands and feeling the engine reverberate in my bones. Irving cleared his throat and climbed the ladder into the wheel-house. I was now alone with Bo Weinberg, whose head had slumped forward in the privacy of his torment and I didn't want to be alone with him so took Irving's place at the bottom of the ladder and started to climb it, rung by rung, but with my back to it, climbing the ladder backwards by my heels and then coming to a halt half-way up between the deck and the hatch, and entwining myself there because Irving had begun to talk with the pilot of the boat. It was dark up there when I peered up, or maybe as dark as the light from a compass or some other dashboard item, and I could picture them staring over the prow from that height as they spoke, looking out to sea as the boat rode to its impenetrable destination.

'You know,' Irving said in his dry, gravelly voice. 'I started out on the water. I ran speedboats for Big Bill.'

'That right?'

'Oh sure. What is it, ten years now? He had good boats. Liberty motors in 'em, do thirty-five knots loaded.'

'Sure,' the pilot said, 'I knew those boats. I remember the *Mary B.* I remember the *Bettina.*'

'That's right,' Irving said. '*The King Fisher. The Galway.*'

'Irving,' Bo Weinberg said from his tub.

'Come out here to the Row,' Irving said, 'load the cases, be back on the Brooklyn side or off Canal Street in no time at all.'

'Sure,' the pilot said. 'We had names and numbers. We knew which boats were Bill's and which boats we could go after.'

'What?' Irving said, and the word seemed conditioned by a wan smile I imagined up there in the dark.

'Sure,' the pilot said. 'I ran a Cutter in those days. The *CG 282.*'

'I'll be damned,' Irving said.

'Saw you go by. Well, hell, even a lieutenant senior-grade only got a hundred and change a month.'

'Irving!' Bo shouted. 'For Godssake!'

'He covered everything,' Irving said. 'That's what I liked about Bill. Nothing left to chance. After the first year we didn't even have to carry cash. Everything on credit, like gentlemen. Yes, Bo?' I heard Irving say from the top of the ladder.

'Put me out, Irving. I'm begging you, put a muzzle to my head.'

'Aw, Bo, you know I can't do that,' Irving said.

'He's a madman, he's a maniac. He's torturing me.'

'I'm sorry,' Irving said in his soft voice.

'The Mick did him worse. I took the Mick out for him. How do you think I did it, hanging him by his thumbs, like this? You think I held him for contemplation? I did it, bang, it was done. I did it mercifully,' Bo Weinberg said. 'I did it merci-full-ly,' he said, the word breaking out of him on a sob.

'I could give you a drink, Bo,' Irving called down. 'You want a drink?'

But Bo was sobbing and didn't seem to hear, and in a moment Irving was gone from the hatch.

The pilot had turned on the radio, twisting the knob through static till some voices came in. He kept it low, like music. People talked. Other people answered. They warranted their positions.

'It was clean work,' Irving was saying to the pilot. 'It was good work. Weather never bothered me. I liked it all. I liked making my landing just where and when I'd figured to.'

'Sure,' the pilot said.

'I grew up on City Island,' Irving said. 'I was born next to a boat-yard. If I didn't catch on when I did I would have joined the Navy.'

Bo Weinberg was moaning the word 'Mama'. Over and over again, 'Mama, Mama.'

'I used to like it at the end of a night's work,' Irving said. 'We kept the boats there in the marine garage on 122nd Street.'

'Sure,' the pilot said.

'You'd come up the East River just before dawn. City fast asleep. First you'd see the sun on the gulls, they'd turn white. Then the top of the Hell Gate turned to gold.'

GRANTA

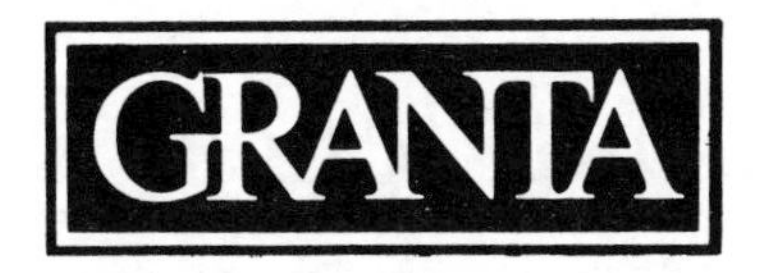

MONA SIMPSON
VICTORY MILLS

Mona Simpson

Katy: Confidence

I have driven a car on acid, carried my mother drunk upstairs and slept with numerous men and one woman to no consequence. I am comfortable in airports. There are things I don't tell, small things of my own. I collect: snowball paperweights from all the cities I've been, buttons, books about birds. I am twenty-five years old and I only left home once and that was a long time ago.

I was, believe it or not, the librarian type. All I really loved to do was sleep. I couldn't get enough of it. Nine, ten hours, and I'd wake up on my belly, lift my arm off the pillow and it would drag a sleeve of dream, green, sequiny, dripping.

That was when I lived a life of trying. I scrubbed floors for money, did homework, checking it over, staying in from the sun. Every step I took seemed dire. Doing things that might be good for me later. I learned things the hard way. I believed in it—the value of work, earning everything, nothing free.

All that changed and came crashing down. I began to hate people for talking, dealing, making bargains, for getting what they wanted from each other.

There were three of us smart in the high school, home in Victory Mills. I'd busted ass all through trying for college in New York City. Then 15 April 1979 comes around and I didn't get in. Grades were supposed to be money we could spend; I had the money and they wouldn't let me buy. I still don't know why for sure. I only applied two places. I suppose I should have done more.

This was still that period when I wouldn't go out in the sun to tan because I'd read about skin cancer and I wanted to keep my skin pure. I wanted to save my whole self, preserve me as if I were a fruit to be eaten sugared in winter, instead of now, summer, ripe, fresh from the tree.

I only mean my body. The outside. I don't mean sex. That went well with work. Other people reward themselves with cookies. I was trampy, but hard-working too. Some prune guidance counsellor maybe wrote me down as slut. The two boys—the black boy I loved and the faggot—they both got in. I'd been waiting all my life. To get in. To get out. It all came raining down around me, touching my ears. It was the outside but it felt like the inside, the way when you run and stop it rushes to your ears like warm velvet.

I had been saving myself for some Kennedy at college. I figured out from the old *Life* magazines in the cellar, one of those red-haired, freckle-faced kids would be about my age. They all went to college. They got in. My life's motto had been: later.

Don't get me wrong. I wasn't saving myself inside. A girl gets horny too. I just didn't want to sunburn or get lines or hurt myself somewhere that would show. Sex I considered exercise.

Not that I made myself pretty. I was a tomboy bad. I didn't want to end up a slave to pretty, like my mamma whose biggest problem in life was keeping her nails long working the second assembly, swing shift at the mill.

It began to change the night I smoked my first cigarette, a Marlboro. I let go. It has to do with dancing. I had no future anymore. I was at the Holiday Inn late, hearing Tray jam with the band. Tray was my boy and he was going. Alex, the faggot, sat there too. Alex asked me to go along to New York City. I figured it would be random from now on. Anyway I wouldn't stay here. And maybe you could get things other ways than trying.

That night I thought of something I'd always wanted. Victory Mills High elects a reunion secretary every May. I decided to be it. I studied the pictures of class officers from 1961 on. I started the next morning campaigning. Everyone else was going for beauty queen. I watched the pretty girls in their ribbon-bonded matching sweaters, sticking to themselves on the top tier of the lawn—they were practising their posture for the crêpe-paper coronation. I went to Penny's and got Peter Pan blouses, a different pastel for every day of the week. I really wanted to be secretary. Betsy, the black Betty Crocker, she was the meanest snob. And I kicked the gravel down by the parking lot smiling at how stupid they were. I talked to everyone, every nerd, every baldy, all the weirdos nobody else would have. It didn't cost to say good morning. Those pretty birdy girls didn't think. Everyone gets a vote, the rejects too.

Alex: Memory

There is something I'll never forget, the day we took the bus down to New York from Victory Mills. Tray and me. Katy came later.

Didn't seem to matter who was going to college anymore. We three were going. We passed outside town, through Schuylerville and on a hill in the country, from an old grey house, sagging above a little makeshift farm, Betsy comes running in her home-made skirt and Peter Pan collar, arms and legs pell-mell, beating hard as an egg-beater, her chest leading, she runs up to the bus and screams.

I looked hard at Tray, leaving her. She was his sweet girl, they did everything the straight way, the date, the pictures, prom.

'I got things to do,' he said, that day on the bus, stern, spitting into his hand.

He didn't end up in school long. He started a band in New York City. And it was going. We turned room-mates, Katy and me. Back home in Victory Mills, Katy was a weird thing. No one knew what to make of her. She and her mom lived in an old house on the slow main street, looking right across into the mill, our beautiful brick mill, founded 1897 and still working. Once a paper mill, now they make cardboard containers. We've all been there once, punched our cards.

Back home in Victory Mills, she wore big blue gym shorts, a kind you can't get anymore, with elastic waist, a yellow border around the leg holes, a high school name on one leg. She lay on her couch with her hair ringed back and taught little boys to lick her after school. It was like lifting a wet baby up to breast and teaching it to nurse. They would sometimes gag and try to bob up but she pushed their heads down. This was in the afternoon, her momma working the second shift across the road at the mill.

I know because I was one of the boys. Alexander Sutter. Best boy in the fourth grade class. I had a nine-year-old Catholic boy crew cut. She wrote on my hair with her finger. I remembered her fat belly, undulation, wetness, long after old man Whipple from the antique store made me his boy, dry and smelling of talcum, dry clothes on dry skin, layers, like old leaves patched on a long autumn road.

I only went to her that once and never back. It was a Friday and I threw up my mother's fish that night. The next morning I showed up at Whipple's door, asking for work as a scout. It was quiet in there, like backstage at church. They had an old radio playing organ. There were two guys. Whipple with his black plastic glasses, and the tall younger one you never saw, who sat in a corner, needling a rug. He hand-hooked rugs. I learned what you called it later.

While Whipple got me the keys to the car, the tall one looked up and said, 'Rouse.'

So they sent me to Rouse, an old filthy broken-down place on Rouse Road. I loved to drive, I'd always known how, driving this hilly, glowing road, like over a body. All that country, a few barns—as far as you can see something warm inside those hills, a ticking, grass and weeds like hair with a breeze in it. All named Rouse.

Rouse must have owned it all once.

But I drove down the long gravel into a house held by termites and a broken-down barn full of old things with no grace, chipped dishes, years of filth, a prodigy of cobwebs, and behind the decrepit desk in the basement a woman worthy of a circus tent, a fat lady sitting under blue light in ruffles and layers of pink make-up.

'Can I help you, young man? What do you collect?'

My eye caught on the chips, the hair-line cracks, damage. I didn't buy anything, and when I climbed out of that basement back to the light, two yapping dogs came at my leg, biting through the denim.

I returned to Whipple with a bloody patch of trouser. He made me take them off to wash, he cleaned the tears with iodine, I got the job as scout and in two months' time, the tall rug-hooker was gone, in an apartment of his own on Lake George, near the amusement park.

I saw him years later, giving a hand-hooking demonstration in a tent at the Washington County Fair.

Katy kept the other boys coming, the neighborhood boys from the fourth grade up through high school. She had them afternoons, before she fixed her own supper and started on her homework. I went over nights after dinner with Whipple. Whipple turned out to be a brilliant cook. He is a very careful person; neat, he measures well. But I left at nine o'clock and walked to Katy.

She didn't like the boys to know she came. It took them years to learn to ask and then she told them no. In fourth and fifth and even tenth grade, she had them all believing it was for them they were doing it. That they were getting something off of her.

You left feeling a mouthful of dust, dust from that couch. You ate dust and a smell entered your clothes. With me that one time, it went on forever, I didn't know how it could stop. I heard the clatter of slow heels on the broken sidewalk, I had a vision of her body severing at the waist, all I had was her legs on either side of me, my fingers on her tummy actually told a ridge, an end of muscle and skin.

Then the five o'clock whistle blew and the shift came out at the mill. I was the only boy that never came back and that turned out for a good reason. I always blamed it a little on her, all of it. Whipple too. I didn't want him then, I was too young and owlish, I was still such a boy. It shouldn't have happened to me then. Maybe I could have been different.

We had something holding us together besides our need for and hatred of school. The faggot and the slut—those teachers hated giving us 'A's, it was like squeezing out pellets.

But we were in love with the same boy. It was a funny class. Three decent students and something wrong with every one of us. She's trampy in her high heels she falls off of, I'm an old man's queer and Tray—the best boy in our high school is black. He didn't look at either of us, except for talking. He wanted Betsy who made her own dresses with little flowers on them. He had a wild life though. I think Betsy always dreamed she could straighten him out, like something under a dumb hot iron. By tenth grade he dealt dope and stayed out all night, learning piano and sax from the guys who travelled and played the Lucky Lounge in the Glenn's Falls Holiday Inn, thirty miles north of Victory Mills.

Katy: Confidence

There is a kind of woman, you've met her, she's real old, 39, 40 or something, fat, no make-up, legs like loose sausages, hair a flat piece of cloth, nothing to draw even a fly to her and she'll tell you a secret, the pride of her solitude—men are threatened by her intelligence.

I used to be the sort of person that believed looking good took lots of time. Shopping got a bad name with me. As if finger-nails took hours. You eat protein, they grow like claws. But it is true. There are drawbacks.

Riding the Greyhound down to New York City I decided in the Albany bus station that this was the last day of my life for doing what I don't really want to do.

No more school. Didn't do me any good anyway. Even things I learned for myself and just liked before, remembered in my minutes off, how a bee flies even though it's physically impossible and all about Andrew Jackson's duel, those seemed tainted now and I was ashamed for what pleasure I took in any of it.

I looked like shit in the bus station bathroom mirror. My hair was mush dead, there were zits around the corners of my mouth, pale skin, I was eating a candy bar, dirty fingers.

First and mostly I wanted all that to change. I wanted to carry myself like somebody. I wasn't garbage and I wasn't going to let anybody treat me that way. I felt a pang for my mother, back in Victory Mills, probably ironing right now, trying in her little ways to keep things up. I remember she told me once how when they spilled acid on her leg at the mill, she made a girl-friend stop at the shoe-store, run in with her last twenty and buy her a new pair of pumps. 'Something neutral and nice,' my mother said, 'with a little heel.' She thought if she looked a little nice, people in the hospital would treat her better.

And then I wanted to act and sing. I knew I wasn't trained for singing. Old Man Whipple, the volunteer choir leader, had to admit I had a voice, but he didn't do anything to teach me. He always looked at me from the corner of his eye, like some horror. But I can act. I could act better than the people who got into college, who had never looked this bad in a cracked Greyhound mirror. I could act better than people who won things.

And I started that day.

Growing up with just a mom, I learned no morals, the way other people did. She understood when I lied or cheated on a school test. She could feel for a person wanting a thing so bad. I used all that in acting. My mamma taught me pity. That's all you need. That's all you need. I said that once before and Tray used it as a refrain in his band. He didn't credit me either, the bum.

On the bus from Albany to New York I wrote my name on the window's steam with my finger, the way I used to on boys' crew cuts, when their hair was soft and short like an otter's.

I was all alone.

My old man was an old, old man who sat in front of the fire all day in the woods, his hands hung down like severed claws, just down in front of him. Even when I went to see him, he couldn't take his eyes off the flames.

Alex: Memory

I come into the 5th Street apartment, my own and only home in New York, turn the key and walk into what should be a Balthus painting. Schubert songs ring off the walls, it's seven o'clock, softly dark outside and not a light on in the place. It's as if nothing works, time stopped, there's some quality of density in the air. The old record-player moves over those sad songs. I flicked the hall light on and went into the living-room. There she was: Katy. And a new guy, one I hadn't seen before. The windows were open and a breeze blowing in, lacy hialanthus leaves netted against the fire-escape. Wind scattered papers—our bills—from the table onto the floor and I sat down in a chair, but they didn't acknowledge me.

Katy—aged twenty-four—lay stomach-down on the couch, wearing only gym shorts, face jammed into the end pillow.

He was kneeling behind her, hovering over her, alert as a cat. One of her knees was bent and her bare calf dallied in the air. He caught her foot, rubbed it, working it between his hands. Then he stopped, squeezed out oil, snuck between her toes, then down her legs, in the cup of her knee, down her thighs.

She seemed floppy to the point of dead, motionless. I didn't worry. I'd seen her like this plenty. It was her state with straight men, with her dates. Sleepy. They were always kneading her, rubbing her, licking her, jamming their tongues into ears, trying to surprise her to interest. She closed her eyes, sank, relapsed, curled down under their fingers. Not what would turn me on. But they massaged her, pummelled her, scratched her, petted her, dug into her neck. whatever she wanted.

And they all helped. Her career was inching up. She got parts. One, the one who braided her hair into a hundred tiny braids, he paid for her singing lessons. She got better. She knew the ones to know.

This is what the men she finds are like—their names are always

Jeremy or Joshua or Eliot. She's never once brought home a Chuck or a Dave. They're usually short, no-shouldered—she likes that—and every one of them so far has worn wire-rimmed glasses.

There was a crack, a scratch in the record. The lights were still out. I sat in my chair, my arms on the arm-rests, thinking how we'd changed. A scratch on a record could make Katy hate her life. I almost found it soothing. I could still hear the music in music. I scouted weekends, I bought a car my sophomore year and drove up Saturday mornings, visited Whipple.

I put myself through college buying antique needlework and Limoges upstate, trotting it in to Sotheby's and selling. I was in graduate school now. As soon as I left New York, I didn't want Whipple to touch me anymore. For a year or two, we had a weird thing when I visited. We'd sleep in the same bed but we never touched, not even accidentally, even an arm. We fell into deep sound sleeps. I began to understand Katy. Now, the tall man is back with Whipple. They're planting a Japanese garden. They still have the best house in Victory Mills.

Katy shifted on the couch with the scratch. Her eyelids open a little.

'Knobs,' she said, her foot wiggling in the air near his face.

Knobs were the hip joints, those ball-bearing-like places in her back and this one knew that. He bent over, greedy, eager, with the silence of a vocation. In the position of a woman kneeling by a river with a washboard, he dug and pummelled her lower back.

She was already successful. She had a running part then, a record contract on an independent label. But still we couldn't imagine in our wildest dreams what she is now. Maybe she could. She had it in her, secret and unfolding all the while.

The apartment was trashed that night. Her prosthetic-looking runner's bra hooked over a chair's arm, empty bottles of selzer on the floor. That's right, this one was a runner. Eliot, I think his name was.

They got up and left it all, went to dinner, her head bent down, mumbling, him massaging one of her hands between his. As they walked, he rubbed her wrists and hands and neck, finally getting her in a taxi and then paying for her food in the end.

'Get your hands off her,' I wanted to say.

I don't know what time she got in. I stayed up late reading

Varieties of Religious Experience. A first edition I took from Whipple. It seemed to mean more, words on pages—the first of something. I didn't hear her come in, but the next morning when I woke I heard her humming *Pomp and Circumstance* and I find her sitting on the closed toilet seat, the bathroom door open, combing her hair. It's wet and the comb leaves carved ridges. I always think her hair looks best like that—wet, dark, combed straight back.

'I don't know what you see in him.'

'You don't see it?'

'There's not much to see.'

'Not everybody's a size-queen.'

'There are two kinds of people in the world. Size-queens and liars.'

'Nooooo. There are girls.' She sighed, looking at her face in profile. 'I've never seen one I couldn't see. It doesn't matter.'

'Not if all you want to do is fall asleep.'

She picked up the blow-dryer, blared it on.

'You're the one who always wants your life to look more like a magazine,' I said. 'So stop doing that to your hair. It looks like everybody else. A million cocker spaniel girls.'

'I want white tulips and marble tables and tarnished silver candle-sticks. I don't mean my hair. My hair can be like everyone else. You're weird,' she says.

'Why do you want to stamp out everything idiosyncratic?'

'It's only looks,' she shrugs, 'I know what works.'

I'm sitting by the window and I hear her move through her closet, hangers jangling on the metal rod, drawers bang shut, the puff and clink of things.

Then I hear her dig through my coin can.

Is it my imagination or do people expect me to pay for things? Me. The graduate student. I stand up and walk so she can hear me.

'The bus,' she calls. 'I'm seeing Tray and the guys jam today. You wanna come?'

'No.' All these years later, I don't want Tray in the state of New York, not to mention in my life.

But sure enough, that's where he is, in my life, in my apartment, that night and many nights for a long long time. Our walls are sheer plaster. I can hear and imagine everything. For the first time in years, she doesn't sleep.

It's rare that I get her alone now. But tonight we ate Chinese noodles by ourselves on the floor. She was distracted. 'He's home in Victory Mills,' she says.

'And you're home here with me. So pay attention.'

'I'm sorry. I'm just—it's hard to only be noticed for your looks,' she says.

'The only thing worse than being wanted for your body is *not* being wanted for your body.'

The saving element in Katy is her grin, it's as fast or slow as a thought—real time. 'Yeah. You're right. I remember.'

The thing about men is, we're not supposed to care about that stuff. We're not supposed to try. Women, they can be beautiful, they should be, we want them smooth. Women talk about buttons and shopping and dry cleaners. We're supposed to just perspire and be.

Have you ever seen a guy who does nothing? Let me tell you something about him. He doesn't look like Cary Grant. You don't remember him. You didn't like him. You hardly even saw him. He reads too many books. He smokes cigarettes. He's attached to black-and-white movies on TV, popcorn late at night with his roommate on the bed. His friendships mean everything to him. He's getting too old for all this, but he doesn't think so. This—this life—could go on forever. He doesn't understand why all the others want to get up and leave.

Katy: Confidence

Have you noticed that when couples are just about to split forever, they buy big things? Houses. Cars. Even boats. If they're poor and they can't buy they make. That's when my parents got me, 1961, Victory Mills, New York, my father a Samsonite man.

I was with the same kids all my life from class to class, year to year, that's the way it was in Victory Mills. Once in a while a kid would move and he'd drop off the face of the earth. Once they were gone, they were forgotten. A girl named Linda wrote me a letter once from Michigan. It was really strange getting a letter. It was the first letter I ever got.

It said things like, 'I quit smoking and making out,' which was weird because she was my friend and I never knew she did those things. It opened up a world like the lid of a trunk.

That was Linda, I could show you her. My room-mate Alex had a framed picture of our second grade class, he can point to each one and tell you what they are doing now, which ones are dead. If he didn't have that, I wouldn't remember what any of them looked like. He's different.

'After the age of twenty-five, everyone you meet is a stranger.' That is a direct quote from Alex. He believes it. Probably one reason he's with me. But I don't think that myself. I think the past is random, as random as anything that happens to you today on the street. You can pick what you want, leave the rest. I've abandoned most of my family. Not my mom. My old man just sits in front of the fire and ruins himself.

They weren't any good for me. I still send a present to my mom every Christmas. I remember her, when I was little, giving me blackjack gum. If there was only one stick left at the bottom of her purse, we'd split it.

The rich people, story books, the conventions—they had it right all along. So that is the way I try to live now. That is why my hair looks like everybody else. But there are drawbacks. You're less dexterous with long moon-filed nails. Today I spent twenty minutes with a knife trying to get the knots out of my sneaker laces. Have you ever thought how knots get *into* sneaker laces?

It is a drawback. Being pretty. Doing it in a way like everybody else. You might say, well, you can get someone else to get your knots out. I've noticed, now, if you say you live in downtown Chicago but you miss the country, people will tell you the country is full of bugs, blackflies, yellow-jackets, bluewhatevers, and that every bar closes at eleven.

People want to talk you out of regret. As if we can't bear to know that there are other lives humming along, parallel.

Alex: Memory

New York City is really 200 people. The rest is done with mirrors.

So come summer, we had to get out. We rented a place upstate. The year had changed us, none more than Katy, who had girls coming up to her even at the Saratoga Springs race-track asking for her autograph.

Tray had a club he was playing downtown with his band and even I had a financial coup. After my orals, an eighteenth-century creweled sampler I found in Rutland ('By the hand of Rebecca Cole, in her Eight year') went for 111 times what I paid for it.

And Katy was in love with Tray. Most of the reason we were back upstate was him. We were following him. But I knew there was trouble, I don't know how I knew. One day I was driving to Hudson to see some pillars and Tray said he'd come along. He was like that with me. He didn't ask.

I had just a faint inkling because he wasn't talking as much to Katy, and a long time ago, I heard Betsy and her family had moved.

In Hudson, Tray told me where to drive and then we saw her—I didn't think I'd recognize her, but of course I did, right away. She stood there on the porch, looking out into nothing specific, into Hudson, her lower lip slung open from time, her body taller and fuller than I'd ever seen it, her breasts more subject to gravity. She looked what we used to call ample. She was more grown-up than we were, she had on a house-dress, sturdy shoes.

One arm hung down by her side, her palm forward. Whipple once told me that was how you knew women from men, the carrier angle of their arms. And her long arm hung open, asking, her other hand clasped it at the wrist.

I remembered those fisted arms beating the morning air at nineteen, chasing the bus, angry, promising, saying, I can keep up, I'll show you.

And now it was all the humility of disappointment, she stood on the porch, not quite looking at us, staring out blank. 'This is what I've become,' she seemed to be saying. 'Take it or leave it,' she said, like a statue.

Rest of the summer, Katy was different. Pretty soon she found an admirer. He was a local caretaker who climbed over the hedge next door and drank tea with her. By August, he was coming through her room window at three o'clock afternoons, so I figured she'd be all right. He's married now, with three kids. The last time I was in Saratoga, I saw him in his green uniform pants, standing by the desk at the library. I walked up behind and heard him asking the librarian for Katy's new album. 'It must be checked out,' the librarian said.

Katy: Confidence

There is no front door into acting. You can't do it a straight way. Regular practice, diligence, graduations from one right school to another, all that is nothing. What would the meant confession of a goody-good be, the jazz of a regular guy, a practicer? Acting is the way we all hurt ourselves and bad. It's not about good habits.

I went to NYU today to give a talk to a class. When I left I stood there at the square, watching the hundreds of students that I never was, carrying books. They came to hear what I said, took notes. Two will write me letters thanking me, at the same time asking for help in some obscure way, wanting to know how they can make it like I did and for sure.

If one of them could give a monologue on his own scheming, how he feels silly doing his exercises alone in a room, trying to scream, but the neighbors, from two to four every day, his terror that he doesn't have the thing, the thing without properties, the invisible, which I know is in me as sure as I have a hand. I like that: The confessions of a schemer. The go-getter's secret terror. But schemers are grudging. All show, no fall down. They'd never tell that.

Still I envy those students with their books. But not for acting.

I am not the first girl men notice. But once they know me, I have them for a long time. I used to say, my open legs are good to fall on. But now I've used that in acting. I've given it words.

When I moved out of the apartment with Alex, I didn't know where I was going. I packed to leave in one morning while he watched me. There was one thing of his I wanted to take and I lifted it off the nail in the wall from where it was hanging over his desk. It was that picture of our second grade class. Alex is so organized. He keeps his things so nice and neat. He can see where to put a picture on the wall.

He was standing there and his face fell. I saw him go old in an instant, loose flesh from the sides of his cheeks fell around his mouth.

'I need that,' he said.

Alex: Memory

They all still come around the house. They want to tell me dirt about her. As if it's not perfectly clear where I stand. I've taken to wearing pedal-pushers when I receive them.

There is much discussion of her hair, the issue of whether the waves, the mess, are real.

I remembered the bald man, Charlie, he'd sit on the toilet seat, she'd be naked on a towel over the floor, weaving braids.

The last one here was the professor, a married man, wearing wing-tips.

'There was one afternoon in this apartment,' he told me, 'I thought, shit, she'd got this place in this funny neighborhood, it was all she could afford then, I suppose. A lot of girls,' (you should have heard him say *girls*,) 'would have taken a smaller place in a nice area, decorated, bought clothes . . .'

'Waited,' I said.

He sputtered out, laughing. 'It was completely empty and I came over to help her paint. We painted for hours, those tin ceilings were a bitch. I sweated. I did the kind of work I'd never done at home.

'There was one wooden chair in the middle of the room.' (He pointed to where I was sitting.) 'Her belt buckle, still in her jeans, knocked on the floor. She was wearing just an old thin blue T-shirt, paint on it, ripped at the neck and nothing else.

'I was on the straight chair, just my fly open, she straddled me, I rocked her from her bare waist, all that hair in front of her face.

'I knew about the others, after me,' he said, 'Kreiser, Bustello. I knew about it. They poured so much money into her.' He swallowed the last of his coffee and put the glass down. 'She did what she had to do. She came up here all alone. Her parents were millworkers. She didn't have any help. She did what she had to do.'

They come here one by one. It's like I'm taking gentleman callers. They tell their lewd stories, looking greedily around the room, I serve them one cup of coffee and then they leave. And I never tell them my story. How quiet she was last year after we came back from the summer Tray married Betsy. I worked on my dissertation, she was in rehearsal, we were like man and wife. The house was running a way houses can sometimes—a good factory, everything comes on time and when you need it.

We jogged together. We steamed vegetables. Her collection of snowball paperweights we lined up on top of a black bookcase. Our secrets were things like two pints of strawberry ice cream with our own spoons at midnight. Once, we went to an old movie (*Easy Money* with Ray Milland at his peak) and made out under the silver light and then when we came home, we went to bed. It was my idea, Valentine's Day, and when I told her I'd never been with a woman since her in fourth grade, I think she felt she had to go through with it. It was easy, an underwater feeling, her skin had a smell I was used to, we slept cradled in each other's arms.

But the next morning, she was standing on a ladder, collecting her snowballs in a bag, leaving. 'I feel like getting married,' was her apology. 'I'm old,' she said.

I still live in this apartment. I've done the foyer in a teal blue copied precisely from a Braque, but nothing in my life changes fast. I still have her great-grandmother's arched slate gravestone—Katy's one attempt at collecting. She came home with it after a weekend with Tray, exuberant, falling over from the weight. 'You took it from the cemetery?' I asked. She nodded, proud. 'Nobody uses it,' she said. 'And I'll look at it. We'll put it somewhere prominent. You figure out where.' We set it on the mantelpiece over the fireplace, our apartment's best thing.

The pushers on our corner still hawk politely, then say, 'Have a nice day, Sir,' when I shake my head no. So the neighborhood hasn't gone yet. I go to Bergdorf's, the clerks hiss at me in my stretch pants, 'Get out if you're not going to buy anything.' I pick up a tie and want to whimper, 'I can afford it, I just don't *like* it.' But here, on Fifth and A, I feel like Mr Man. 'Have a nice day, Sir.' *Sir*.

I'm smoking as I walk west, past the low lighted houses,

looking up in the windows, the way people in New York always must, where you can partially see.

Katy lives in a house like this, behind solemn brick, she'll be in bed now, dusk, late afternoon, the time when it's still light outside but too dim to read or see clearly in rooms. The air outside turns blue, brighter blue, inside, shades of grey, the thick sheets around her in folds, the furniture still and large beyond her bed, she sinks down turning, her hair a weight, a tickle across her bare back. She hugs the baby, they mould to each other like that and begin turning in the grey, as the outlines of buildings in the window soften and with a sound like pouring, sifting sand, they turn together, letting themselves loose, allowing footsteps below at the faint edge of hearing. And then there is a streak of pleasure through her breast down her thigh, the elastic push and pull, the exact gasping, they are falling, his feet curl under her hand, they are feeling themselves fall asleep.

I put out my cigarette under my shoe, wipe my hand on my jeans. They are not thinking of me tonight. Tray is home where we came from, Katy and her baby bob asleep somewhere in the sky, and I am out again walking the night streets towards a party, a thin man, eager, believing myself the same boy who came here years ago, unchanged, still waiting.

A year later, I finally see her again. It's been that long. She used to phone me, we'd meet at her house, at a restaurant, I'd write back a postcard, something witty and old, and I wouldn't hear from her again for about eight months. I'd leave messages. Letters. No answer. Then she calls and it's exactly the same again. I began to feel guided, she runs the timetable, she even moved the conversation. Aren't we cool talking about our love-lives last, long after careers and old friends. Moms and Dads.

We never mention Tray. Not with the baby. Never. I have no idea what the husband thinks. Barry.

I'd had it. I stopped calling, stopped postcards, this year I even missed Valentine's Day, which is—for a certain kind of swish-fag I've become—a national holiday. I had one picked out too, thirties violets, brown letters. Forget it. I gave it to the fat lady who runs the cheese shop downstairs.

Then her momma died. All those years of smoking. I heard it from Whipple and went right home. She died on a leaf weekend in New England, I couldn't get a car, I took the bus up. It was a rainy day, misty rain, and we were all there in the cemetery. Whipple, Brad the rug-hooker and me in good dark suits. There were lots of people from the mill, neighbors. I didn't know anymore who they all were. She came in from the city carrying her baby through the cemetery, her good high heels ruining in the grass.

I'd seen her in the city, years of winters, carrying her shoes in little plastic grocery bags, wearing her sneakers into fancy parties, hiding them in the lobby.

She'd driven up in a Mercedes, a car as big and dry as a boat. She stood there, after, fastening the baby into the seat and Whipple bends over and asks her to tea. For my surprise, she says she'll come. She and Whipple were never fond.

'Where's your husband?' Brad says.

'Not here.' She's still fussing with the belts on the baby-seat.

And then right there, at the edge of the cemetery, cars pull up, a line of headlights through the fine rain. Mothers wait, hands on steering wheels. Pre-teen girls run out and clamour at her with their open autograph books, vinyl-covered affairs with little gold locks the way diaries used to be when we were that age.

'I think I'm busy doing something,' she said, not taking her eyes off Roy. Then she closed his door, locking it, and walked around to the other side, them tugging at her. 'I've got a wet child,' she said.

At Whipple's, they served us a real tea. They used everything they'd always had wrapped and hidden and behind glass. Tea and hot milk from the silver samovar with Russian eagles, Sèvres cups and saucers, perfect heavy Georgian spoons. Hot buttered scones, *crème fraîche*. Katy took her shoes off and set the baby on the floor. He was still a baby but just the end of it, becoming a little boy. She asked for a blanket and got a love-chain Amish quilt and took out her canteen of equipment and started changing him. We all stared. I'd never really seen a baby changed before.

Roy is a beautiful child, one eye blue, one eye green. I'd often day-dreamed, walking alone down Manhattan blocks, her tragic death and my inheritance. I imagined the phone calls, the men knocking at my door. Husband and wife on the same plane . . .

I'd made myself cry when the truth was I wanted to steal him. But now, watching her patient, quick fingers move with thoroughness, impersonal purpose, the shit, wiping more of the shit, so a smear streaked the edge of her hand, I turned away. My stomach flipped over once. I didn't want any of it anymore. It was not for me. Not what I wanted. When I looked back, Whipple and Brad were still staring. Their manners slipped off them. We forgot the order, the tea, the food.

Katy and I were alone a little later when the men moved to the kitchen. All the finery had to be washed and wrapped and put back. The baby was clean now and a baby again, the boy I day-dreamed of, and Katy and I hung our heads over the carpet. We really hadn't seen each other much for a long time.

Of course, Tray wasn't here and I was, like always. Like the night ten years ago they crowned her beauty queen and Tray didn't come because Betsy was home crying. Tray could have made her safe today, rescued it by showing for one hour. Me, the whole day, gave only a consolation. I knew that, she knew that. I didn't like it. It felt an embarrassment. Why was I still here if I couldn't do more?

Her daddy wasn't there at the cemetery either. He was bad off. He'd been living out in the woods in a little cabin years now, hardly talked to anybody. I guess that's what people do after the big social events—the parties, the weddings, funerals. They sit around counting who came and who didn't.

'You know what I found?' She showed me a letter in a yellowed envelope. Whipple sold old letters mixed in with the box of postcards.

'From my mom to my dad accepting his proposal.'

'Proposal,' I said. I scanned the letter. 'If you want me, OK,' she had written. 'You know what you are getting. You understand that my heart is tired. I will try to help us to be happy. But please believe that a part of me is already given away, thrown away, gone forever.'

I was stunned. I read on. I didn't want to but I smiled. Her heart had been broken by a man, she said, named Rudy. This had been seven years earlier.

'When was this?' Then I looked at the postmark. Victory Mills, 1949.

'Who is Rudy?'

She shook her head. 'Some guy. Some guy in the world. I don't know. I found it in the basement. I think of it as this trickle of green water, here'—she motioned one hand over her chest.

I asked Whipple if there had ever been a guy named Rudy around here. Somehow, I pictured him in New York City. But I was wrong. Whipple and Brad were giving each other sliding, funny looks, Katy and me turned in bewilderment until Whipple said, 'I was Rudy. That was me. Rudolph's my middle name. They called me Rudy till I was thirty.'

'Did you know that?' Katy went at me like an accusation.

'I never knew till this minute.' I looked at Whipple. 'You never told me June was in love with you.'

He shrugged and rustled, preened a hand through his thin hair. 'She wanted to marry me and have children. I could have been your father. But it wouldn't have been you. That was June and your dad. It was a long time ago, I don't remember much. It was nothing that mattered. Just when we were kids.'

Katy nodded. It was true. She folded her mother's letter up to save it.

'Were you actually lovers?' This wasn't for Katy anymore. She had her son in her arms, she was rocking, touching the bottoms of his feet so they pulled up back into him, a reflex. She looked ready to go.

This was for me. I was interested.

'Not really. She was, I guess, more than me. It was a one of those.'

'But did you sleep together?' I had a photograph, a little snapshot of A.R. Whipple in his twenties. He was a pretty boy, the kind of boy a girl would fall for. Of course, he'd never looked like that since I knew him. I stole the picture once from Whipple long ago.

'Oh, yes. A year almost. She was my first and my last woman. I thought for a while—I don't know. I broke it off with her and I did the right thing, I'm sure of it. I couldn't have. Not like that.'

And it was still raining outside, shining and dulling spots of the Japanese garden.

I wanted to talk about it more, all night, I had a thousand questions, but it was Katy's mother and Katy wanted to go now. I helped her into her car. Inside she turned the heat on and it hummed comfortable as a room. We strapped the baby in, carefully, struggling his socks over his heels. The others had the sense to leave us alone.

'Don't you want to stay, Katy? Aren't you curious about what really happened? It's your family.'

She shook her head. 'No one remembers right. We'll never know.' She laid her hands on the steering-wheel and pushed her shoulders up. Her head fell. The steering-wheel was bound in pale leather and she bit it, held it in her mouth. I slid down next to her, rubbing her shoulders, rubbing both sides of her neck. Her eyes closed, her lips loosened. That was all.

GRANTA

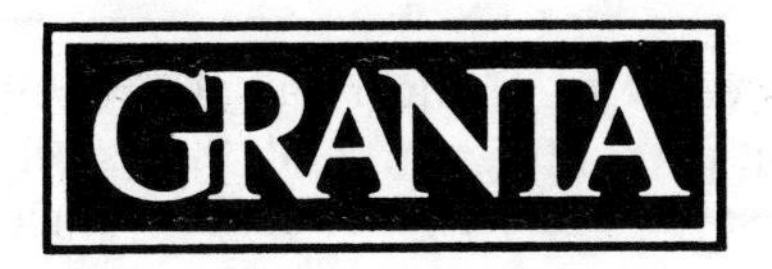

Jay McInerney
The Business

Like everybody else, I'd heard all about Hollywood before I moved out here. Still, you think things will be different for you. You say to yourself, sure this is a jungle, but I'm Doctor Livingstone.

I graduated from Columbia with a degree in English Lit. and went to work for a newspaper in Bergen County, just across the river from Manhattan, keeping my cheap apartment on West 111th Street where I lived with my girl-friend. My thesis was a post-structuralist tome on film adaptations of major American novels, and within a year I'd wangled the job of movie reviewer and entertainment reporter. I loved the movies—always have. The idea of being a screen-writer came to me during a pool interview with a writer-director who was in Manhattan flacking for his new picture. It wasn't the fact that he didn't seem particularly bright or that he made his ascent sound so haphazard and effortless. It was the way he looked, sitting there, smoking a cigarette as the light coming through the window of the forty-floor corporate tower hit his face: I could see the pores in his skin and the stubble of his beard and there was something green stuck between two of his teeth and I suddenly thought—I could be there, sitting where he's sitting with two days' growth and a green thing on my teeth.

I didn't quit my job that day, but I started writing screenplays, renting the films I loved and studying the structure, thinking about what they had in common. I was encouraged in this by my Aunt Alexis, who had once been a contract player at Paramount. She'd been in a couple of westerns with John Wayne and was briefly married to a director. After her divorce she moved to New York—the director made her quit the movies and it was too late to go back, she said, but she still talked as if she were a member of a warm, extended family called 'the business'. She claimed some tolerably famous names as friends, and avidly studied *Variety* and the *Hollywood Reporter*. I knew from the family that she'd been somewhat badly used by 'the business', but she wasn't bitter. She gave acting lessons in New York, occasionally did community theatre. When I'd moved to New York, she more or less adopted me. My parents were divorced, fading into the orange sunsets of Arizona and Florida respectively.

Alexis lived in thrifty elegance in a splendid pre-war building over near Sutton Place, a duplex she'd occupied for years, the first couple of them with her third husband, and which she wouldn't have been able to afford if not for rent control. Even with a severely depressed rent she'd had to subdivide the apartment and sublet the more luxurious lower floor, which was separated by two doors from her own quarters upstairs. The centerpiece of the downstairs apartment was a spectacular canopy bed replete with rose-colored chintz drapery. Alexis herself slept in the upstairs parlor on a pull-out sofa and cooked on a hotplate, since the kitchen was downstairs. At this time the lower floor was occupied by the manager of a rock group who was burning holes in all the upholstery. Alexis knew because she snuck down whenever he wasn't home and snooped around. She was trying to decide what to do: she needed the rent, plus she had introduced this guy to the landlord as her nephew, since he refused to let her take a subtenant.

Alexis encouraged me in my screen-writing ambitions and read my earliest attempts. She also gave me the only good advice I've ever gotten on the subject. 'Dalton Trumbo once told me the secret of a screenplay,' she said, mixing herself a negroni in the closet which served her as kitchen, pantry and bar. It was six in the evening and the fading light was slicing through the mullioned windows at a forty-five-degree angle—that second-to-last light which is thick and yellow with doomed bravado—making the dust swimming through the big old apartment seem like movie mist.

'He was a lovely man, much misunderstood,' she said. 'That McCarthy stuff—terrible. But as I was starting to say, Dalton said to me one night—I think we were at the Selznicks' and I said, "Dalton, what's your secret?" and he whispered something in my ear which I won't repeat. I gave him a little slap on the wrist, not that I was really mad. I was flattered and told him so, but at the time I was still married to the fag. This was before I found out he was that way. So I said to Dalton, "No, no, I meant—what's the secret of a great screenplay?" And he said, "It's very simple, Lex. Three acts—first act, get man up tree, second act, shake a stick at him, third act, get him down from the tree."'

When Alexis was really in her cups she told me she'd call up Sam Cohn or some other great friend of hers and fix me up, the exquisitely carved syllables of her trained speech softening, liquefying like the cubes in her glass. But the fact is she didn't have any juice in the industry. I didn't mind. I eventually landed an agent on my own, at which point I figured it was time to make the leap of faith. Plus my girl-friend announced that she was in love with my best friend and that they'd been sleeping together for six months.

I sublet my apartment in New York and got a place in Venice three blocks from the beach. It was February and I loved it, leaving the frozen, rotten city for a place where I could wake up smelling flowers and the ocean. At the same time, Venice of all places in Southern California reminded me of New York—everything had a certain shabbiness, and there were bums all over the place. The crime rate was pretty impressive, just so I wouldn't get too homesick—just so I'd know I was on the same planet. But basically I felt the same way about California that Keats did about Chapman's *Homer*. I quit smoking, got on the Pritkin diet, started sleeping regular hours.

One thing I didn't do was rush out to join AA, which was just becoming the really hip thing to do then. If I had I probably would have met some girls. But I was still under the thrall of the idea of the writer as holy lush. Who could imagine Raymond Chandler sober? One of my favorite Hollywood stories involved Herman Mankiewicz, the other genius behind *Citizen Kane*. Mankiewicz found himself one night in the home of one of Beverly Hills's newest *nouveau riche* hostesses, a woman who had recently learned the correct sequence of forks and knives for a seven-course dinner and who took this knowledge very seriously. The legendarily unmanageable writer arrived for dinner drunk and got drunker, till finally he evacuated the contents of his stomach all over the dinner-table. As the guests looked on horrified, Mankiewicz turned to his hostess and said, 'Don't worry—the white wine came up with the fish.'

In Venice I had a little terrace off the back of my second-storey studio. I'd wake up early most mornings and take my computer out there to work. It overlooked a tiny courtyard choked with cactus and palms and flowering bushes. I grew up in the intemperate zones and I still get a little thrill when I see a palm tree. My landlady believed that nature should be allowed to take its course and she just let it all grow. The couple across the courtyard believed in nature too; they fucked at all hours with the shades up and I couldn't help seeing them, usually her bobbing up and down on top of him, facing me. I guess she was performing. Maybe she thought I was a casting director—all the world's a couch. Anyway, I appreciated it. That was as close as I was getting to carnal knowledge.

My second screenplay opens with this very scene: close on couple making love, girl on top, camera pulling back out the window, pulling back, reverse angle on the guy watching this scene from the terrace across the way. Eventually the girl and the guy on the terrace meet and have this incredible affair. She decides to leave her boyfriend for him, the writer, but of course the boyfriend turns out to be a coke dealer involved with some very heavy Colombians, and it turns out the girl knows a lot about the inner workings of the gang and has information that could implicate the boys in a murder. Except she doesn't know it . . .

Believe it or not, this screenplay attracted the interest of a fairly important producer. That was when I first met Danny Brode. The producer had a first-look deal with the studio where Brode was the new vice-president of production. Brode scheduled a meeting for me—my first with a studio executive. I spent about three hours in the morning trying to figure out what to wear and whether or not to shave. Finally I shaved and put on a white shirt, tie, blazer and jeans. Brode made me wait an hour and finally, when I was ushered into his dazzling white office, he shook my hand and said, 'What, you got a funeral or a wedding to go to today?' and when I looked baffled, he said, 'The tie, dude.' So I knew I'd worn the wrong thing and I knew he knew I'd worn the tie for him.

Brode was wearing jeans and a work-shirt which barely held him in. Standing about five foot six, the man weighed 350 if he weighed an ounce. He could have been a sumo wrestler. If his cheeks had been breasts they'd have filled D-cups, and his chin would have made another man's pot belly. Not exactly the guy to be handing out advice on appearances. Anyway, he told me he'd been running late all day and could we take the meeting in his car: he had to drive out to the valley to check on the mixing for a film in post-production.

So we go out to the parking-lot and get in his car, which is this four-door Maserati sedan. I didn't even know Maserati made sedans but I figured Brode was too big to drive around in their sports model—maybe they made it especially for him. We drive out to the valley and he spends most of the time on his carphone, but in between he listens to me pitching like crazy. Finally he says, 'Instead of a writer, how about if this guy is an artist? We move the thing from Venice to San Francisco, and the guy's got this big like studio full of canvases and he sees the couple screwing from his studio. The art thing is very hot right now, and we'll get a lot more visuals this way.'

I don't know, I probably would have made my hero into a female impersonator; I was dying to get into the game. I'd exhausted my savings and my Subaru needed new brakes and I hadn't met a girl yet who wanted to go out to dinner with an unemployed screen-writer. My ex-best friend had just written to say he and my ex-girl-friend were getting married and he hoped I didn't have any hard feelings. I pretended to think about Brode's suggestion deeply for a minute and then I said, 'I like it. I think I could work it.'

He dropped me at the gate of the sound studio and gave me a card with the number of a car service. 'We'll work it out with your agent.' I stood around for an hour baking in the sun waiting for the car which finally came and took me back to the studio. I bought a bottle of Spanish bubbly and knocked it back on the terrace that night while my neighbors traded orgasms.

I called Alexis in New York. She told me that I was now part of the big, happy family which was the business, and we talked for an hour to the accompaniment of her ice cubes tinkling in the crystal highball glass.

I thought about calling my old girl-friend: in my drunken state I could imagine her chagrin when she realized what she'd given up. But I passed out instead.

'Martin, darling, I'm going to make you a rich man,' my agent told me a week later. She'd grown up on Long Island and had only been out here a couple of years but she talked just like something out of *What Makes Sammy Run*—they must give you a copy at LAX Arrivals or something; I don't know why I didn't get mine.

The deal was three drafts at scale, which wasn't a great deal but it was more money than I made in a year at the newspaper and I was thrilled. Plus, it was a foot in the door. 'Danny Brode is really big,' my agent said without a trace of irony. 'That man is going places and he can take you with him.'

'I don't want to go to the fat farm,' I said.

'You better start watching your mouth around this town,' my agent said. 'It's a small community and if you want to be part of it you've got to play by the rules. Bo Goldman and Bob Towne can maybe afford to be smartasses but you can't.'

'Could you send me a list of the rules?' I said. I was so happy I couldn't help being full of myself. The next week my agent took me to lunch at Spago's. She introduced me to several people she described as important players, calling me 'Martin Brooks, the writer'.

Then I started writing. I wrote a draft making my hero into a painter. I flew up to San Francisco to get atmosphere, talked to gallery-owners and artists. Just dropping the name of the studio was enough to open doors. I implied that a major star was interested in the lead. Back home I was able to get an interivew with a narcotics squad investigator for the LAPD who filled me in on the inner workings of the drug cartels.

Ten weeks after the papers were signed I handed in a draft. The next day I got a package Federal Express—a bottle of Cristal attached to Danny Brode's business card. That was how it was printed on the card: Danny Brode. Just an ordinary guy, right? No need to wear a tie here. Anyway, drinking that bottle of Cristal was the high point of the whole experience. The hangover set in a couple of weeks later.

My agent called. 'Basically they are thrilled with the script. Absolutely ecstatic. But they want to talk to you about a couple of tiny little changes.'

I said, 'No problem, we're contracted for three drafts, right? I mean, I make another ten grand or something for a rewrite, don't I?'

'Don't worry your genius brain about it. Just take the meeting and we'll see what they want.'

What they wanted was a completely different story. Brode had fallen in love with his idea of the art world backdrop and now he wanted to make it a movie about the way commerce corrupted artists. Columbia had a project about the art world in development and he wanted to beat them. We could keep the drug element—the big shot gallery-owner would be involved in the coke trade. I sat in his huge white office, trying to figure out where the white walls and the white leather furniture began and ended, trying to see the virtues of his new idea, trying to recognize some shred of my own script.

I nodded like an idiot and said it sounded really interesting. I practically told him he was a genius and that I didn't know why I hadn't seen his idea in the first place. Back home, though, I got mad. I called my agent and screamed at her about the stupidity of studio executives and about the way art was corrupted by commerce. She listened patiently. Finally I said, 'Well, at least I get paid to be a whore.'

She said, 'Try and pick out the virtues in his concept. I'll work on the money.'

'What do you mean, "work on the money"? It's in the contract.'

'Of course,' she said.

I sat down again trying just to be professional about the whole thing, which is to say, trying not to give a shit. Three weeks later I delivered the new draft. I'd just bought a new car, a little Beamer, with my first check. One morning when my agent called me to talk about another project, I said, 'When am I getting paid for my second draft?'

'We're calling that a polish instead of a draft.'

'What do you mean, a "polish"? It was a whole new story. I knocked myself out. Are you trying to tell me I'm not getting paid? What about the contract?'

'Look, Martin. You're new at this. Brode says it's a polish and he wants you to do one more polish before he shows it to the big man.'

I was beginning to understand. I'd already been in L.A. a year. 'You mean I get paid for a second draft, but it's not a draft unless fat Brode says it's a draft.'

'Let's just say it behoves us to please Danny Brode at this point and give him some slack. Believe me, darling, you don't want to get known as a difficult writer. Give him one more polish and I promise you it will be worth your while in the long run.'

I threatened to go to the Writer's Guild and she said she would hate to end our professional relationship, but I had to trust her on this one.

Maybe you've heard the one about the agent who's approached by the Devil. The Devil says, 'I'll give you any client you want—Redford, Newman, Pacino, you name it—in exchange for your immortal soul for all eternity.' And the agent says, 'What's the catch?'

I stopped trusting my agent from that moment on, but I followed her advice. I wrote a total of three drafts and got paid for one. The project was in turnaround within six months. I didn't see Brode for a couple of years but my agent was right, in a sense. That deal led to others—even though my first baby died, I was bankable; I'd had a deal and that led to other deals and within a couple of years I had my first movie in production and I'd moved into a place in Laurel Canyon, although I continued to sublet the place in Manhattan, maintaining a tie to my pain and to a world which still seemed more real than the one in which I lived. And whenever I needed a villain for a story, someone rich and powerful to harass the leads, I was always able to draw on my impressions of Danny Brode.

Brode became even more rich and powerful over the next couple of years. He married the daughter of a major Hollywood dynasty and shortly thereafter was running the studio which the family controlled. Consolidation of power through marriage was established procedure in this particular family and on one side they were related to one of America's major crime syndicates. Brode's father-in-law was alleged to be responsible for some untimely deaths, and in the film community it was whispered that a premarital conference had been held in which Brode had been made to understand that if he ran around on his wife, he would fall precipitously from grace. This was considered bizarre, since everybody fucked around in proportion to their power and wealth, people who ran studios and owned casinos most of all. I mean, that was practically the whole point of being successful. But the old boy was apparently over-fond of his first daughter.

'Some nice Faustian elements in this situation,' I said to the lunch partner who first filled me in on this story. I once heard someone say there are only seven basic stories, but in this business there's only one. In Hollywood the story is always Faust.

'Some nice who?' my lunch partner said.

I said I was just thinking of a German film.

Brode got even fatter. In a town where everybody had a personal trainer and where a green salad was considered a main course, there was something almost heroic about his obesity. I saw him sometimes at Morton's or wherever, and after a while—I'd say from the time CAA took over my representation and I started dating actresses—he even began to recognize me. I heard stories. My first agent was right—the bitch. It's a small town.

One of the stories I heard was about a novelist I knew from Columbia. After his first novel made him famous, he star-tripped out here to soak up some of the gravy. Success came on him pretty quickly and he ran so fast to keep up with it that he got out in front of it. He bought a million-dollar co-op on Central Park West and a beach house in Maine, plus he had a little problem with the 'C' word. He'd sold his book to Brode's studio outright, which is to say he got paid the same no matter whether it went into production or not. By the time the second payment was due, this writer was pretty desperate for money—he was overdue on both his mortgages, his girl-friend had an insatiable wardrobe and his wife was socking him for a big settlement. Brode knew about this. So when it came time to pay off, he called the writer up to his house in Malibu and he said, 'Look, I owe you a quarter mil, but at this point I don't know if we're going to go into production. Things are tight and your stock's down in the wine-cellar with the cabernets. Let's just say I either could give you seventy-five and we could call it even. Or I could tie you up in court for the next ten years.' The writer started screaming about the contract, his agency, the Writer's Guild. And Brode said, 'Talk to your agent, babe. I think he'll see it my way.'

Even in Hollywood this was not standard procedure, but the writer's stock had dropped: after being hot for a season, he'd cooled off fast, and the agency, after a lot of thought, decided to go with Brode and advised the writer to take the seventy-five and shut up.

By the time I heard this story, I wasn't even surprised. I'd learned a lot in three years.

I did well by local standards, and it wasn't surprising that I found myself doing business with Brode again. Several production companies were interested in an idea of mine when Brode called my agency to say he wanted to work with me. CAA packaged a deal with me, a director and two stars. The story was set in New York. This was the one I'd been wanting to do from the beginning. Let's just say it was a story of betrayal and revenge. The one-liner on the project, devised by my agent, was: 'A Yuppie *Postman Always Ring Twice*.' For a variety of reasons, some of them aesthetic, it was important to me that the movie be shot in New York. Brode wanted to do it in Toronto and send a second unit to New York for a day. It was a money issue; Toronto was cheaper.

I knew I didn't have the juice to change anybody's mind when two or three million dollars were at stake, so I worked on the director. He was a man with several commercially successful films behind him who was dying to be an *auteur*. He wanted the kind of respect that Scorsese and Coppola got and he didn't understand how it had eluded him so far. An autodidactic actor had recently introduced him to the work of Dostoevsky—an author I should check out, he assured me, Russian, as a matter of fact—and within weeks it had worked a change on his demeanor: he had grown a beard and started scowling. It wasn't difficult to convince him that the New York critical and intellectual fraternity would take his film much more seriously if it were *authentic*—that is to say, if it were shot in New York. I said you couldn't fake these things, not even in the movies. Look at Woody Allen, I said. You think he'd shoot a movie in Toronto? You think they'd publish him in the *New Yorker* if he did?

That did it. Brode kicked and screamed, but the director was adamant and very eloquent on the subject of authenticity. And in Hollywood directors count. In the end, after I'd given them my third draft, they headed off to New York with long lines of credit and suitcases full of money for the friendly local teamsters.

I flew out for pre-production; the director had decided he liked having me around and Brode had no objections; so long as I didn't ask for a consulting fee, they were happy to pay my expenses in New York. Brode's assistant, a woman named Karen Levine, would be on location, while Brode would fly out once in a while to check in. Levine was petite, blonde and terribly swift and efficient so that at first I hardly noticed her. In Los Angeles one can become accustomed to thinking of beauty as something languid, sexiness as a quality that inhered in the slow-moving, self-conscious forms of actresses and professional companions. Karen was no odalisque. But I started noticing her more and more. Despite the legendary informality of Southern California—the indiscriminate use of first names, the gross over-extension of the concept of friendship—it was unusual to encounter a human being who sailed straight between the whirlpool of craven servility and the shoals of condescension. Karen did and I liked her for it. It occurred to me that she was doing more than working for Brode, but I inquired discreetly and the buzz was that they were strictly business and that Brode was living up to the terms of his contract with his father-in-law.

When I heard Karen say she was looking for a place in New York for the three months of filming, I thought of Alexis, who had finally thrown the rock manager out of her first floor and lost several thousand in the process. I figured the studio could afford a rent high enough to make up some of what Hollywood had taken out of her in the old days, and I knew Alexis would be thrilled by her new proximity to 'the business'. Plus I liked the idea of doing Karen a favor.

I brought Karen over one afternoon. We were both staying at the Sherry Netherland, and I walked her over to Sutton Place. I wanted her to see New York at its best—she'd grown up in Pasadena and was a little nervous about the idea of three months in dirty, dangerous Manhattan. It was a cool day at the end of April. The air was crisp, swept clean by a light breeze. Across the street the Plaza glowed white in the sun. We went up to 60th and across to Park Avenue, where the daffodils were blooming in the center median and the doormen stood guard at the entrances of the grand old buildings, then over past Bloomingdales and down to 57th. Karen looked casually tremendous in an Irish sweater and jeans. I felt like a boy returning to his own country having made good in the colonies, although I eventually learned that the two people I most wanted to impress had moved to Cambridge.

Alexis greeted us in a flowing caftan, kissed Karen on both cheeks and ushered us into the upstairs parlor where she'd laid out a tea service that would have done Claridge's proud. Karen was impressed. Alexis took us on a tour, pointing out the treasures—pictures of herself and the Duke, herself and Bogie, a signed first edition from Faulkner, a set of candlesticks given to her by Red Skelton, the love seat on which she'd traded confidences—here she winked—with Errol Flynn. Some of this stuff I hadn't even heard before. She was laying it on a bit thick, but Karen managed to seem both attentive and relaxed. Then we went downstairs and I knew Karen was hooked as soon as she saw the big canopy bed, floating in the middle of the panelled bedroom, wreathed in rose-colored chintz, like a feminized pirate galleon.

Before Alexis had mixed her second negroni—'I don't usually drink in the afternoon but this is an occasion, are you sure you won't have one?'—it was decided. Karen would move in for three months. Alexis would introduce her to the landlord as her niece. When we finally left at six, I asked Karen out to dinner. She said she had a lot of work to do but she'd love to some other night.

Shooting started. I hung around, visiting the set every couple of days. Brode flew in almost every weekend, which surprised me. He seemed to be taking an excessive interest in the project. Each visit he managed to make someone miserable. Three weeks into shooting it was me. He had decided he didn't like the ending as it stood in the script and he wanted me to rewrite it. He wanted something more upbeat. I kicked and screamed and told him about the integrity of the story. I tried to go through the director, but Brode had worked on him first, and he was impervious to my warnings about what the *New Yorker* would think of the new ending. Apparently he was thinking about his two points of the gross.

'It comes down to this, Martin,' Brode told me as he sawed into a veal chop at Elaine's one night. 'You write the new ending or we hire somebody else. I'll give you another twenty-five; call it a consulting fee.' I watched him insert half a pound of calf's flesh into his maw and waited for him to choke on it and die. It occurred to me that he was too fat for anybody to perform the Heimlich manoeuvre on him successfully. I could say to the police officers—hey, sorry, I tried to get my arms around him but no go.

I rewrote the ending. For me it ruined the movie but the public bought almost a hundred million dollars' worth of tickets and I was nominated for an Oscar the next spring.

I visited Alexis frequently and used these occasions to knock on Karen's door. One night she let me take her to dinner. I told her about my ex-girl-friend in New York, how she'd run off and married my best friend. I'd never told anyone before. Karen was appalled and sympathetic. She'd adopted the uniform of feminine night-time New York, looking very sexy in a small, tight black dress. At her door we exchanged a long, encouraging kiss, but when the kiss began to develop a life of its own, she pulled back and said she had to be up at five.

One evening I went over to visit Alexis. As she was mixing two negronis, she said, 'Who's Karen's boyfriend, anyway? I take it he's some big shot.'

'I don't think she has a boyfriend,' I said, somewhat alarmed.

'I can't understand how someone as pretty as Karen could let that fat man touch her.'

Feeling relieved, I said, 'That wasn't Karen's boyfriend, that was her boss.'

Alexis snorted. 'Call it what you want. I know about girls and their bosses.'

'It's not like that with Karen,' I said.

'Don't tell me what it's not. I have to listen to them. And now I have to buy a new bed.'

'What are you talking about?'

She put a finger to her lips, walked over to the stairway door, opened it and listened. Then she motioned for me to follow her down.

The canopy bed was wrecked. The satin-skirted box-spring, which had previously seemed to float above the floor, was now earthbound; the bedposts and the chintz draperies were tangled and splayed.

'Her boss,' Alexis said, sounding for once as tough and as cynical as someone who has been hard-used by men and their institutions, as someone who has had to sing and dance for her supper and then some, revealing in those two syllables the bitterness and anger that I always thought she would have been entitled to feel. 'I've had bosses like that,' she said, her eyes distant, looking back in time. After ten or fifteen seconds in which I contemplated the grotesque implications of the wreckage she shook her head and smiled. 'But thank God I never had one that gross. Poor girl's risking her life every time she climbs into bed with that whale.'

Brode had flown back to the West Coast that morning, so I had a whole week to think out my strategy. When he got back to town, I called a meeting. The only time he could meet me was breakfast. He told me to meet him over at the Regency at seven-thirty, the Regency being at this time where all the big players from L.A. stayed when they were in town, and where the local robber barons and power-brokers breakfasted. When I arrived at eight, he was just finishing off a plate of ham and eggs.

'I'm just leaving,' he said. 'What's up?'

'I want to do another movie. I think you might like this one.'

'What's the pitch?' he said. 'I've got exactly three minutes.'

'It's a mob story,' I said.

'Pretty well-worked turf,' he mumbled.

'You'll like this,' I said, fishing in the bread basket to retrieve a piece of toast which Brode had somehow overlooked. I leaned back in my chair and surveyed the room, rotten with titans of industry and finance and entertainment. It was easy to pick out the movie people—the others wore Hermes ties under bespoke suits of discreet cut and color. Brode was partially covered by a blue Oxford cloth shirt, open three buttons down to expose a wedge of black hair and white flesh. I caught the eye of a local mogul whose expression betrayed aesthetic outrage at Brode's physical appearance and for a moment I found myself on the fat man's side. At least, I thought, Danny Brode looks like what he is. His fellow diners were almost to a man bloated in every way but the obvious one. They'd all made their deals with the Prince. And I saw that I had been too hard on my adopted home town, and realized that I would not be coming back to New York except to visit. For the first time I could remember, I identified myself with the business from which I derived my livelihood, confederate with Brode and all of the unabashed and unbuttoned men of the West, the land-grabbers and gold-diggers and claim-jumpers and deal-makers, all the restless self-seekers trampling their brethren underfoot in their rush to the beach-front property of the Pacific. These men knew that there was only one story, even if they didn't know who Faust was.

But I had a story of my own to tell.

The story I pitched to Brode concerned a young mobster whose career takes a fast turn for the better when he marries the daughter of a major don. But there's a catch. The don tells him if he ever screws around on his daughter, he'll be a very sorry scuba diver, fifty feet under without oxygen. After the marriage, the new family member does very well. But it seems there's this young wise guy within the organization who happens to live in the same building as this very attractive girl . . .

The story had a sort of farcical scene involving a broken bed. The broken bed led to very dire consequences for some of the parties concerned.

Brode scratched the congealing egg yolk on his plate with the tines of his fork as he listened to the pitch, his pink face taking on color with each sentence. At the end he looked into my eyes to see if he might be mistaken about what he was really hearing.

Then he said, 'What do you want?'

'I want to do another movie with you. OK, maybe not this one, but something else. And I want to produce.'

'I could have you . . .' He didn't finish.

That was how I became a producer. In the end we came to terms that were very satisfactory from my point of view. I don't think Brode felt it was the best deal he'd ever made in his life. I knew that I'd have to watch out for him. But the project I eventually wrote and produced made money for both of us, which made me feel a little safer when I went to sleep at night.

A year later I flew back to New York for Alexis's funeral. One of ten mourners, I cried when they lowered the coffin into the ground out in the cemetery in Queens. The last time I could remember crying was on a day that should have been happy for me. I'd just gotten a call from an agent in California who read my script and decided to represent me. I waited two hours for Terry, my girl-friend, to come home from work. I bought flowers and champagne and called everyone I knew. Finally Terry got home and I almost knocked her over. We'd talked about moving to California together if things worked well for me. I poured champagne on our heads and talked about our future in the promised land.

'We can live near the beach,' I said, following her into the bathroom where she rubbed a pink towel back and forth across her dark hair. 'We'll have a car and we'll drive up to Big Sur on the weekends.' That was when she told me she'd been sleeping with my best friend. One minute I've got champagne streaming down my face and the next minute tears, looking at pink lint from the towel in the dark strands of my girl-friend's wet hair. I thought about that as I listened to the words of the minister at the cemetery. I remembered that day years ago in a one-bedroom apartment on West 111th Street as being the last time I cried. I don't think it will happen again.

GRANTA

LETTERS

Pictures

To the Editor:

I am disturbed by the use of photography in the excellent short article on Beirut by Fawwaz Traboulsi (*Granta* 23, Home). Some of these photographs are intrusive and exploit the suffering of the people depicted in them. I don't understand why they are used at all, but expect that their supposed purpose is to bring home the horror to a country that has not experienced it. But we have imagination. Images of war can be as de-humanizing as the war itself. Show us the living people of Beirut, not their dead. This is a private pain, and is expressed much more deeply and effectively by *Guernica.* Would you want your friend or relative's dead body displayed in a magazine?

Ann Gowland
Surrey

To the Editor:

Two weeks ago, an Israeli soldier lay dying in a street in Bethlehem, shot in the head. Television pictures showed the ghouls from the international media standing over him, taking photographs! That you, as publishers, should, through your photographs of Beirut, seek to turn your readers into similar ghoulish voyeurs is a disgrace.

The writing accompanying the photographs linked Beirut with Guernica, and Israel with fascist Spain; it did not mention that Lebanese had been murdering Lebanese for years before Israel invaded.

Were those poor civilians you depict really killed by Israelis? More likely they were the victims of fellow Lebanese—whether 'Christian' Phalangists, Moslem Hezbollah or Druze Militia—or any of the other myriad, murderous factions in that mad place.

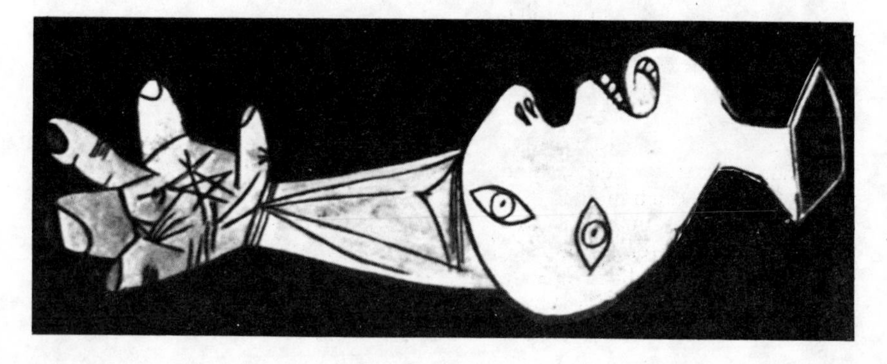

Guernica courtesy of The Prado, Madrid

I subscribed for the likes of Milan Kundera, Italo Calvino, Gabriel García Márquez—not for Palestinian propaganda!

Philip Roberts
Wrexham
Clwyd

Privacy

To the Editor:

I read Ian Hamilton's 'J.D. Salinger *versus* Random House, Inc.', (*Granta* 23) with growing disgust. If Salinger says clearly that he wants 'no more intrusions on his privacy,' then any subsequent attempts to quote or paraphrase extensively from his private and so far unpublished letters can only be a blatant, gross invasion of his privacy. It is unfortunate that Salinger's lawyers chose to defend him through largely inapplicable copyright laws.

As a journalist, I am familiar with the conflict between privacy and the public interest; my trade has its share of guttersnipes who do not hesitate to behave like Mr Hamilton, but at least most know what they are: they do not stoop to speciously high-minded apologia in the 'quality' press.

The public interest is an elastic concept, but usually involves some tangible benefit to a broad sector of the public. Does Salinger's literary hoard qualify? Of course his writings are of literary interest, but do we need to know *now*? Could we not wait until the material became decently available?

The only possible motive for Mr Hamilton's extraordinary behaviour was to make money and fame for himself and his publishers.

Tim Sharp
Chiang Mai
Thailand

All letters are welcome and should be addressed to the Editor, Granta, 44a Hobson Street, Cambridge CB1 1NL, England.

Notes on Contributors

Bruce Chatwin's most recent book is *The Songlines*. A new novel, *Utz*, is published in the autumn. His work has previously been published in *Granta* 10 and *Granta* 21. **Anthony Cavendish** is a former employee of the British Government. He now works in banking. **Philip Roth**'s most recent novel is *The Counterlife*. 'His Roth' is the prologue to an autobiographical work, *The Facts*, that Farrar, Straus and Giroux publish in November. **Peter Carey**'s most recent novel is *Oscar and Lucinda*. In July he begins work on a film with Wim Wenders. 'Fortune' will be included in **Tobias Wolff**'s childhood memoir, *This Boy's Life*, to be published next year by Atlantic Monthly Press in the United States and Bloomsbury in Britain. His novella *The Barracks Thief*, winner of the PEN/Faulkner Award, appeared in *Granta* 8. **James Fenton**'s collection of his Far East journalism *All the Wrong Places* is published in the autumn. These pieces originally appeared in *Granta* 15, *Granta* 18 and *Granta* 22. **Nik Cohn** is the author of *Awopbopaloobopalapbamboom*, a history of rock 'n' roll, and *Rock Dreams*, a collaboration with Guy Pellaert. A collection of his fiction and journalism, *Ball the Wall*, will be published next year. **E.L. Doctorow** is the author of *Ragtime* and *The Book of Daniel*. 'The Apprentice' is taken from a work-in-progress, a novel titled *Billy Bathgate*. **Mona Simpson** is the author of *Anywhere But Here*. **Jay McInerney**'s new novel is *Story of My Life*, published in England this August and in the United States this September. He is currently working on an investigation into the Robert Chambers 'preppy' murder trial. *Ransom*, his last novel, is currently being made into a film.